BISH BASH
BOSH!

YOUR FAVORITES
ALL PLANTS

BISH BASH
BOSH!

HENRY FIRTH & IAN THEASBY

WM
WILLIAM MORROW
An Imprint of HarperCollins*Publishers*

This book is dedicated to you.
Thanks for picking it up.
We hope you love it.

For information, address HarperCollins Publishers, 195 Broadway,
New York, NY 10007.

HarperCollins books may be purchased for educational, business, or
sales promotional use. For information, please email the Special
Markets Department at SPsales@harpercollins.com.

Originally published in the United Kingdom in 2019 by HQ, an imprint
of HarperCollins Publishers.

FIRST U.S. EDITION

Photography: Lizzie Mayson
Food Styling: Frankie Unsworth
Prop Styling: Sarah Birks
Design: Paul Palmer-Edwards
Creative Director: Louise McGrory
Editorial Director: Rachel Kenny
Senior Commissioning Editor: Kate Fox
Project Editor: Laura Herring
Production Controller: Stefanie Kruszyk

Printed and bound in the USA

Library of Congress Cataloging-in-Publication Data has been applied
for.

ISBN 978-0-06-291121-6

19 20 21 22 23   LSC   10 9 8 7 6 5 4 3 2 1

Contents

Welcome 7

This book 10

Your kitchen 12

Fantastic feasts 16

Bonus recipes 20

Plan your meals 24

1 **QUICK** 26

2 **BIG** 66

3 **FEASTS** 110

4 **SIDES & SHARERS** 148

5 **GREENS** 184

6 **DESSERTS** 212

7 **BREAKFASTS** 256

Eat the rainbow 278

Gratitude 280

Index 282

Welcome

Your favorite food. All plants. Sorted.

Whether you're after a quick midweek meal, you need to satisfy those comfort food cravings, or maybe it's the weekend and you want to cook a full roast dinner to impress the in-laws, we have all your favorite recipes covered. We even have the solution for when only the most decadent chocolate cake will do . . .

Whatever your go-to, all-time favorite dishes, we'll show you how easy it is for them to be plant-based and still be just as delicious—and we think even tastier!

We'll share our tips for making plant-based cooking simple, with recipes to fit around your lifestyle. This book contains everything you need to get you eating more plants, every day. You'll learn how to prepare unbelievable curries, discover our bangin' burgers, and enjoy cheesy pizzas and we'll even let you in on our secret recipe for irresistible finger-licking Wild West Wings. As well as sharing our amazing cakes and desserts. You'll discover loads of new favorite recipes, family feasts, healthy meals, and all-time classics.

Everything is set out to help you nail your cooking, so you can find a recipe that works for you whatever you feel like eating, and however much time you have. We'll show you how to make your food taste amazing and look incredible. And, of course, everything is all plants.

Whether you are a veggie, vegan, or veg-lover looking for new recipes or to cut down on the amount of meat you eat, we've got you covered. Plants have never tasted this good!

BISH, BASH, BOSH!

We are so happy to have you here in our kitchen! This book is all about you. We've poured our life and soul into this, our second cookbook, for just one purpose: to help you enjoy even more plant-based deliciousness in your life.

Looking back over the past five years, it's incredible to think how much our lives have changed.

Back then, both of us were in a pretty bad place. We were running a tech start-up and things weren't going the way we'd hoped. Long hours and money worries were causing us both incredible amounts of stress. We were friends who worked together in the same team, and we were feeling truly worn down by the grind. Something needed to change.

After deciding to cut out all animal products, we can honestly say we both felt the benefits almost overnight. We felt lighter, had more energy, and felt truly rested for the first time in ages. Plants had saved us!

As lovers of food since an early age and passionate home cooks, we went on a voyage of culinary discovery. And for the next few years we dedicated ourselves to sharing everything we learned about how to make delicious plant-based meals, putting all our tried-and-tested recipes online. And with that, BOSH! was born.

Soon after, we published our first cookbook, and in three years we went from home cooks to bestselling authors with videos that have been watched over a billion times. It's been an incredible time for plant-based food and we're so proud to have played a part.

But our work and passion doesn't stop there! We want *even more* people to see the amazing benefits of eating more plants—both in how you feel and in the positive impact it has on our environment. Plant-based eating not only does you good, but it does the planet good, too.

BISH BASH BOSH! is all about making your life easier. We'll join you in the kitchen every step of the way, showing you how to prep and cook with ease. It's about cooking wonderful meals, with recipes that are really easy to follow and deliver amazing results every time.

x Henry and Ian

This book

In this book, we share all our secret recipes and techniques for cooking incredible meat-free meals with ease. We'll teach you how to nail your prep, ingredients, and method in true BISH BASH BOSH! style.

BISH

This book is a celebration of how you can enjoy all your favorite meals using only plants, whether you need a quick meal after a long day or a feast for a party. Whatever the occasion and however much time you have, we have the perfect recipe for you.

Choose from weeknight favorites like Super-Speedy Spaghetti or One-Pan Pasanda. Or try our amazing I-can't-believe-it's-plants dishes like Pulled Jackfruit Sandwich or Faux Gras. Feed a crowd with our incredible curries (see page 16), Seaside Roll, or Holy Trinity Louisiana Gumbo, or there are the always reliable British comfort-food classics, like BOSH! Bangers with Incredible Mash and our delicious Shepherd's Pie.

BASH

Each recipe is broken down into three parts to make it super-easy to follow: ingredients, a prep list of things to have ready like boiling the water or preheating the oven, and a step-by-step method that includes all the prep so you can do it all as you go along.

You'll also find loads of practical tips to make your prep easier, including ideas for making recipes ahead of time and ways you can adapt recipes to work with what you've already got in your cupboards.

We'll teach you the basics of meal planning and meal prep, and show you how to eat the rainbow. You'll also find some brilliant visual indexes to help you navigate the book. Fantastic Feasts will give you inspiration for your favorite dishes—maybe you feel like Italian tonight or you're craving Tex-Mex. And there are dozens of Bonus Recipes like our fail-safe Quick Onion Gravy, BOSH! Quick Custard, and Homemade Melty Cheese, as well as all our favorite dips, sauces, and sides. These key recipes provide a reliable and versatile toolkit for anything you want to create in the kitchen.

BOSH!

We want the recipes in the book to help make you feel great simply by eating amazing food, filled with delicious flavors, that's all plants. The recipes are high in fiber and filled with color, nutrients, and joy. You'll discover a new world of flavor and feel lighter, freer, and happier in your body and your self.

This book will help you make plant-based meals fit easily into your everyday life, however often you choose to cook them.

Welcome to BISH BASH BOSH!

Your kitchen

Get your cupboards and cook space organized, and invest in some essentials, and you'll save yourself loads of time in the kitchen while improving your cooking significantly.

FOOD

Keep a well-stocked pantry for meals in minutes. Here are our suggested essentials—top them up whenever you're running low:
balsamic vinegar | basmati rice | coconut milk | dried rice noodles | dried pasta (whole-grain is healthier) | lentils | ground flaxseed | mixed nuts | mixed seeds | olive oil (extra-virgin for dressings and normal for cooking) | peanut butter (store-bought or keep a stock of your own, see page 266) | all-purpose flour | plant-based milk (fortified with B12) | canola oil | soy sauce | canned beans | canned chickpeas | canned tomatoes | tomato paste

A collection of dried herbs and spices will give you a toolkit of flavor. A great starter selection would be:
black pepper (in a grinder) | pepper flakes | cinnamon | coriander | cumin | curry powder | fennel seeds | oregano | rosemary | thyme | garlic powder | garam masala | ginger | turmeric | hot chili powder | mixed Italian herbs | onion powder | paprika | sea salt

We put greens with everything, so get in the habit of bringing fresh herbs, fruits, and veggies home on a regular basis. We like:
apples | avocados | bananas | berries | basil | carrots | chilies | cilantro | eggplant | garlic | ginger | kale | lemons | limes | mushrooms | onions | oranges | parsley | bell peppers | potatoes | salad greens | spinach | tomatoes

We've always got butter and cheese in the fridge just like we did before, except now they're dairy-free! Our regular fridge items include:
dairy-free butter | dairy-free cheese | dairy-free milk | egg-free mayonnaise | firm tofu | plant-based yogurt

KIT

The number-one piece of equipment we recommend investing in:
If you're going to be cooking more plant-based meals then we really recommend getting a good-quality, high-powered blender. With one of these you can make creamy sauces, nutrient-filled smoothies, homemade milks, and more. And high-powered means high-powered. You want a recent model that's really powerful, with a big jar. If your blender isn't powerful enough to make a completely smooth milk from soaked cashew nuts, get a new one. Trust us, you'll be glad you did.

Here is our list of kit essentials:
sheet pans and baking sheets | cutting boards | colander | fine grater or Microplane | foil | food processor (and/or stick blender) | skillet | heatproof bowl | kitchen timer | knives—at least 3 good-quality ones, plus a sharpening steel | measuring cup | measuring spoons | mixing bowls | saucepans—including some good nonstick ones—with tight-fitting lids | sieve | slotted spoon | spatula | storage containers (we prefer glass) | tongs | vegetable peeler | weighing scales | whisk | wooden spoons

We also love to have:
garlic press | box grater | grill pan | oven-to-table serving dishes | rolling pin | tofu press

COOKSPACE

Organize Your Kitchen, Pantry & Spice Cabinet

We advise you, as over-the-top as it may sound, to label your cupboards and shelves. You can use sticky notes, masking tape, or even get a label-maker for twenty-five bucks. Take everything out of your cupboards and off the shelves (food, crockery, pans—everything) and organize it again. Choose a system that works for you and the amount of stuff you own.

Here's how we organize our kitchen:

Breads & Snacks | Flours & Baking | Herbs & Spices | Miscellaneous | Oils & Vinegars | Nuts & Seeds | Pasta, Rice & Grains | Syrups & Sauces | Cans & Jars

Pro Tips: We like all our food stored on open shelves (not in cupboards) so we can see what we have at a glance | Put a blackboard or notepad on a wall (with chalk or a pen) for noting down ingredients you need to restock

Organize Your Cookware, Equipment & Crockery

Having your workspace well organized will help you be speedy with your cooking and make sure you always know where everything is, so you're never reaching to the back of a cupboard for a spoon when you should be stirring your sauce on the stove. Here's roughly how we organize our bits and bobs.

Near where you cook:

Cutting Boards | Cooking Oils | Food Processor | Knives & Sharpening Steel | Blender | Pans | Pan Lids (in a separate drawer from pans) | Salt & Pepper | Utensils (hang them for easy access) | Weighing Scales

Not so near where you cook:

Cleaning Stuff & Garbage Bags | Foil, Parchment Paper & Freezer Bags | Glasses & Mugs | Measuring Cups & Mixing Bowls | Plates & Bowls (cereal, wide, and serving) | Storage Containers (store with lids on)

Pro Tips: Get your family, friends, or roommates on board with the system (we use a coffee-buying punishment for disobeyers) | Update your system from time to time as your collection grows | Stacking boxes and labels can be really useful for expanding your kitchen in an organized way

Fantastic feasts (and where to find them)

Whatever you're in the mood for, we've got you covered! Fancy some spice? Then check out our Incredible Curries. In need of a health boost, then we have an Eat the Rainbow selection of recipes just for you. Or maybe you want to know how to make plant-based versions of your favorite British classics? Let these collections of recipes inspire you!

ITALIAN FLAVORS

Here's a selection of our favorite Italian-inspired dishes, with a BOSH! twist.

Super-Speedy Spaghetti (page 32)
Margherita Pizza (page 102)
Classic Lasagna (page 112)

INCREDIBLE CURRIES

This spread of Indian-inspired dishes will spice up any dinner party! Pick your favorites and enjoy a culinary trip across the Indian subcontinent.

One-Pan Pasanda (page 28)
Ian's Delightful Daal & Roti (page 70)
Curry House Jalfrezi (page 74)
Sweet Potato Tikka Masala (page 88)
Henry's Biryani with Cilantro Chutney (page 121)
Big Bad Bhajis with Spicy Tomato Chutney (page 169)

SOUTH-EAST ASIAN DELICIOUSNESS

The deep and warming heat of Thailand, Vietnam, and Malaysia comes out in this wonderful selection of dishes.

Tom Kha (page 35)
Vietnamese Sticky Tofu (page 36)
Bún Bò Huế (page 68)
Satay Summer Rolls (page 158)
Spicy Thai Salad (page 190)

16

TAKEAWAY CLASSICS

Summon up delights from your favorite Chinese and Japanese restaurants with this little selection. Healthy, tasty, and full of umami.

Singapore Fried Vermicelli (page 44)
Eggplant Katsu (page 57)
Speedy Hoisin Mushrooms (page 64)
Sushi Cupcakes (page 153)
Bang Bang Noodle Salad (page 201)

CHRISTMAS & THANKSGIVING

The most wonderful time of the year is even better when enjoyed with these incredibly hearty dishes. This selection is what our Christmas could look like, but you can enjoy it as a Sunday roast any time of the year.

Ultimate Nut Roast (page 128)
Christmas Crisscross (page 134)
Brussels Sprouts with Maple Mushrooms (page 137)
Bangers in Blankets (page 137)
Perfect Gravy (page 143)
Notella Christmas Tree (page 252)

EAT THE RAINBOW

If you're looking to fill your body with color and nutrients then these dishes will see you right. Get your greens and colors in with this feast of plant-based goodness.

Broccauliflower Cheese (page 54)
Roast Sweet Potato Tagine (page 98)
Mega Mezze Platter (page 194)
Crunchy Carnival Salad (page 205)
Healthy Meal Prep (page 206)
Nuevos Rancheros (page 265)

HIGH PROTEIN

Where do we get our protein? From plants!
These dishes pack a protein punch so you can
munch down knowing that you're giving your
body what it needs after a big gym sesh.

Vietnamese Sticky Tofu (page 36)
Faux Gras (page 39)
Ultimate Falafel Wrap (page 77)
BOSH! Bangers with Mash & Quick Onion Gravy
   (page 95)
Pan-Fried Seitan Steak with Secret Sauce (page 116)
Nuevos Rancheros (page 265)

BRITISH CLASSICS

Nothing beats a trip around the UK's classic
dishes. Here's a selection of our favorite meals
and pub classics.

Tofish Finger Sandwich (page 83)
Mini Mushroom Pies (page 91)
Pulled Jackfruit Sandwich (page 92)
BOSH! Bangers with Mash & Quick Onion Gravy
   (page 95)
Shepherd's Pie (page 108)
Classic Victoria Sponge (page 245)

TEX-MEX

If you like your chili spicy and your avocados
smashed, then we've got you covered!

Guacajacks & Homemade Chili Oil (page 47)
Quick Quesadillas (page 48)
Holy Trinity Louisiana Gumbo (page 80)
Loaded Potato Nachos with Sour Cream,
   Quick Salsa & Green Chili Guacamole (page 154)
Nuevos Rancheros (page 265)

I CAN'T BELIEVE IT'S PLANTS!

Plants can be super-versatile and we've re-created some of our old favorites in an all-plants style. Check out this selection and see if you can tell the difference!

Faux Gras (page 39)
Piri Piri Chorizo Bake (page 60)
Seaside Roll (page 115)
Pan-Fried Seitan Steak with Secret Sauce (page 116)
Party Poppers (page 165)
Notting Hill Patties (page 173)

MEDITERRANEAN GOODNESS

Here's a load of deliciousness from in and around the Mediterranean. Packed with earthy spices and robust and fresh flavors.

Turbo Tortilla (page 31)
Greek Gyros (page 58)
Piri Piri Chorizo Bake (page 60)
Ultimate Falafel Wrap (page 77)
Spinach & Ricotta Zucchinioli (page 193)
Romesco Salad (page 202)

AMERICAN CLASSICS

We've traveled all over America and compiled our favorite dishes to share with you. You'll feel like you're in *Grease* while chowing down on dishes from this selection.

Wild West Wings (page 160)
Party Poppers with BOSH! BBQ Sauce (page 165)
BBQ Beans with Mushroom Burnt Ends (page 170)
Texan Potato Salad (page 174)
Crunchy Cali Slaw (page 177)

Bonus recipes

There is a whole host of extra deliciousness hidden in this book in the form of mini-recipes that are contained within the main ones. Turn to this collection of go-to basics and fail-safe classics whenever you're looking for a quick custard or a marinara sauce, a tasty dressing or an awesome dip to BOSH! your daily cooking.

DRESSINGS, SAUCES & GRAVIES

Hot Sauce
(page 161)

Katsu Sauce
(page 57)

Pesto
(page 193)

Homemade Sambal Chili Sauce
(page 208)

Quick Onion Gravy
(page 97)

Piri Piri Sauce
(page 60)

Satay Sauce
(page 158)

Café de Paris Secret Sauce
(page 117)

Red Wine Gravy
(page 127)

Bang Bang Peanut Dressing
(page 201)

BOSH! Burger Sauce
(page 50)

Speedy Tartar Sauce
(page 84)

Herb Oil
(page 127)

Homemade Chili Oil
(page 47)

Tomato Sauce
(page 102)

DIPS, CHUTNEYS & SALSAS

 **Cilantro Chutney** (page 122)

 **Green Chili Guacamole** (page 155)

Homemade Turmeric Hummus (page 208)

 **Lemon & Cilantro Hummus** (page 196)

 **Mint Raita** (page 107)

Quick Aioli (page 178)

 **Quick Salsa** (page 155)

 **Salsa Verde** (page 115)

Quick Red Onion Pickle (page 107)

 **Tzatziki** (page 58)

 **Black Bean Guacamole** (page 47)

 **Spicy Tomato Chutney** (page 169)

 **Baba Ganoush** (page 197)

BOSH! HACKS

Balsamic Onions
(page 50)

Carrot Crackling
(page 92)

Cheese: Cashew Mozzarella
(page 102)

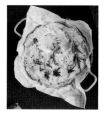
Cheese: Dairy-Free Camembert
(page 150)

Cheese: Melty Cashew Cheese
(page 43)

Eazy Chorizo
(page 61)

Eggplant Bacon
(page 258)

Hash Browns
(page 51)

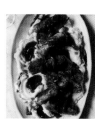
Incredible Mash
(page 96)

Mashy Mashy Peas
(page 84)

Mushroom Burnt Ends
(page 170)

Scrambled Tofu
(page 258)

Sour Cream
(page 155)

SOMETHING SWEET

**BOSH! Quick
Custard**
(page 233)

**Soft Whipped
Cream**
(page 249)

**Vanilla
Buttercream**
(page 245)

**Candied
Peanuts**
(page 248)

Caramel Sauce
(page 217)

**Chocolate
Buttercream**
(page 238)

**Notella
Chocolate
Hazelnut
Spread**
(page 252)

**Chocolate
Syrup**
(page 248)

**Raspberry
Syrup**
(page 249)

Quick Icing
(page 214)

**Raspberry
Sauce**
(page 218)

Plan your meals

Meal prepping is becoming increasingly common. It involves planning and cooking a few meals in advance, which saves you loads of time during the week. Some people like to cook enough food for the entire week, but we prefer to keep things as fresh as possible, so we prepare just a couple of days' worth in advance.

We love meal planning and prepping for a number of reasons:

- It gets rid of the annoying "what's for dinner?" question, reducing the risk of you making unhealthy choices because you're hungry on the way home.

- It helps keep food costs down and reduces waste because all your food is accounted for—and it stops you buying expensive convenience food and frozen dinners!

- You can take full control of your mealtimes and ensure you're eating healthy, nutritious food.

In this book there are lots of great recipes that can be prepped entirely ahead, such as the salads, curries, and pasta dishes, plus plenty more where you can prepare sauces and sides in advance, leaving you only the main meal to make on the day.

Enjoy the freedom from wondering what you are going to eat, make better choices, feel awesome, and eat low-cost, high-flavor and nutritious food.

BISH, BASH, BOSH!

Here's how to meal prep for a week, in three easy steps:

1 Plan your week
Think about your week ahead and decide which meals you'd like to make. Make a note of the recipes you've chosen and the days and times you plan to eat them.

Next, carefully read the recipes you want to cook and identify the areas you can prep for. Some recipes can be part-cooked—for example our pasta sauce on page 209—and you can also make dips, roast veggies, and cook grains and make some dishes all the way to the end so that they can just be reheated on the day.

Plan your prep. We prefer to cook just a couple of days' worth of food in advance, but you might like to prep for more days or even a whole week. Make a note on your meal planner of what you need to prep for each dish—and don't forget to work out how many people you're cooking for each day and adjust the quantities in your recipes accordingly. Then make a shopping list of all your ingredients.

Decide which days you'll be cooking on. We find it easier to get our ingredients online so that we can get everything delivered on the day we prep our meals.

2 Think about how to store your food
Get some airtight containers with tight-fitting lids to store your food in (we prefer glass over plastic) and make sure you have a bag that will fit the containers if you're taking them to work. It's also a good idea to clear some space in your fridge.

3 Cook your food
Now you're ready to actually prep your food! Afterwards, store it in airtight containers in the fridge (make sure to let hot items cool to room temperature before you chill them). Don't forget to label them if you think you might forget what's in each one.

On the day, finish off the dish or reheat it—and don't forget to take your lunch with you to work!

Check out pages 206–9 for a two-day meal plan of delicious recipes.

QUICK

Henry's favorite
Piri Piri Chorizo Bake

Ian's favorite
Guacajacks

ONE-PAN PASANDA

With this wonderful, Anna Jones–inspired recipe you can have
a gorgeous, creamy curry on the table in minutes. Or serve it
alongside some of our other curries, such as the jalfrezi (see page 74)
or our tikka masala (see page 88). If you are cooking a few, get this
one in the oven first then lower the heat as you finish off the others.
Remove from the oven and stir in the yogurt.

SERVES 4

1 head cauliflower (about 1 lb)
1 lb carrots
2 tbsp vegetable oil
a big pinch of salt
a big pinch of black pepper
1 tsp red pepper flakes
1 (13.5 oz) can full-fat coconut milk
½ cup almond flour
¾-inch piece fresh ginger
2 garlic cloves
1 tsp ground turmeric
1 tsp ground cumin
1 tsp garam masala
½ tsp chili powder, optional
7 oz green beans
9 oz coconut yogurt
⅓ cup sliced almonds
¾ oz cilantro

Preheat oven to 350°F | Roasting pan | Grater

First prep and cook the veg | Trim the cauliflower and break it into
1¼-inch florets | If your cauliflower has a lot of good-looking leaves,
reserve them to add to the dish near the end | Trim the carrots and cut
them into 1¼-inch chunks | Spread the vegetables in a roasting pan and
drizzle with the oil | Season with big pinches of salt, pepper, and the red
pepper flakes | Toss to coat the vegetables with the oil and spices | Put
the pan in the oven for 15 minutes

Meanwhile, pour the coconut milk into a mixing bowl | Add the
almond flour and stir | Peel the ginger by scraping off the skin with a
spoon then finely grate it | Peel and grate the garlic | Add the ginger,
garlic, turmeric, cumin, garam masala, and chili powder, if using, to the
bowl | Stir everything together until it's really well mixed

After 15 minutes, take the pan out of the oven and pour the coconut
paste and green beans over the vegetables | Put the pan back in the
oven for 20 minutes, until the cauliflower pieces have started to blacken
at the edges | 10 minutes before the end of cooking, add any reserved
leaves, if using

Remove the pan from the oven and stir in the coconut yogurt
| Season to taste and add more chili powder if you like a hotter curry
| Sprinkle with the sliced almonds and cilantro and serve

TURBO TORTILLA

This is our take on the classic Spanish omelet. It's a great way to use up leftover cooked veggies, so feel free to use whatever you have—just aim for about 14 ounces in total. If you want to up the protein content, replace 3½ ounces of the veg with crumbled firm tofu.

SERVES 4

7 oz waxy new potatoes
3½ oz broccolini
3½ oz asparagus
1 red bell pepper
3½ oz cherry tomatoes
1 medium red onion
1 garlic clove
1 fresh red chili
3 tbsp olive oil
1½ cups chickpea flour
1 tbsp salt
¾ cup water

Preheat oven to 350°F | Large saucepan | Large sheet pan | Large skillet | Medium skillet

Wash and thinly slice the potatoes and put them into the saucepan | Fill the pan with cold, salted water and place over high heat | Bring to a boil and cook for 10 minutes | Drain and set aside

Meanwhile, prepare the rest of your veg | Trim the broccolini and asparagus and cut them into bite-sized pieces | Cut the bell pepper in half, cut out the stem and seeds, and chop into bite-sized chunks | Spread the broccolini, asparagus, bell pepper, and tomatoes evenly over the sheet pan | Put the pan in the oven to cook the veggies for 20 minutes

Peel and thinly slice the red onion and garlic | Rip the stem from the chili, cut it in half lengthwise, remove the seeds, and finely chop | Put the large skillet over medium heat and add 2 tablespoons of the olive oil | Add the onions and sweat, stirring occasionally, for 8–10 minutes, until translucent | Add the garlic and chili and cook for 3–4 minutes more | Remove from the heat and set aside

Sift the chickpea flour and salt into a large bowl | Gradually add the water, whisking constantly until you have a smooth batter (you may not need to use all the water) | Tip all the cooked vegetables into the batter and stir to cover

To cook the tortilla, put the medium skillet over medium heat and add 1 tablespoon olive oil | Pour in the batter with all the vegetables and cook for about 20–25 minutes, until the edges are golden and crispy

Gently loosen the edges with a spatula or spoon and remove from the pan, cut it into slices, and serve immediately | We love to serve this with a little arugula on the side

SUPER-SPEEDY SPAGHETTI

If you're looking for a really quick and easy spaghetti dish, then look no further! Everything goes into the same pot and the water the pasta cooks in then becomes the sauce. It's saucier than a typical pasta, but it's quick, easy, and delicious and we love it!

SERVES 4

1 small red onion
2 garlic cloves
5 tbsp olive oil, plus extra for drizzling
1 tsp salt
14 oz cherry tomatoes
½ tsp chili flakes
2 tbsp red wine (or red wine vinegar)
4¼ cups boiling water
14 oz spaghetti
a handful of black olives (we like Kalamata)
black pepper
¾ cup fresh basil leaves

Large saucepan with a lid over medium heat | Boiling water | Fine grater or Microplane

....

First make the tomato sauce | Peel and thinly slice the red onion | Peel and grate the garlic | Pour the olive oil into the saucepan | Add the sliced onion and salt and fry for 5–7 minutes, stirring occasionally, until the onion is soft and translucent | Add the garlic to the pan, stir it in, and cook for 2 minutes more | Add the tomatoes and stir them around for 2 minutes, until the skins start to split | Sprinkle with the red pepper flakes and pour in the wine, stirring to coat the tomatoes

Pour the boiling water into the pan | Add the spaghetti, let it soften, and then move it around with tongs in the pan until it's well submerged | Put the lid on the pan, turn up the heat, and bring to a boil | Take off the lid and cook at a rolling boil for 10–12 minutes, moving the pasta in the water fairly often to ensure it cooks evenly (it's easiest to do this with tongs)

When most of the starchy water has been absorbed by the pasta, taste to make sure it's cooked to your liking | Quickly slice the olives and stir them into the pasta

Divide among bowls, drizzle with olive oil, and grind over some black pepper | Garnish with the basil leaves and serve

TOM KHA

A gorgeously spicy coconut soup straight from the streets of Bangkok. Try switching out herbs or flavors to make use of what you've got in the fridge. Swap the onions for shallots, green beans for bean sprouts, cilantro for Thai basil . . . Play around and see what works, just keep the base of spices and herbs consistent.

SERVES 4

2-inch piece fresh ginger
2 lemongrass stalks
4 large shallots
1 lb mixed exotic mushrooms
1 red bell pepper
12 oz cherry tomatoes
5 bird's-eye chilies
3½ oz green beans
2 (13.5 oz) cans full-fat coconut milk
7 kaffir lime leaves
¾ cup water
3 tbsp soy sauce
1 tsp coconut sugar
¾ oz cilantro
2 scallions
2 limes

Large saucepan

First prep your veg and aromatics | Peel the ginger by scraping off the skin with a spoon, then thinly slice | Peel the hard outer bark of the lemongrass, roughly chop the tender stalk into three pieces, and bash with the heel of a knife | Peel and thinly slice the shallots | If they're big, roughly chop the mushrooms into bite-sized pieces, otherwise leave them as they are

Cut the bell pepper in half, cut out the stems and seeds, and cut the flesh into 1-inch chunks | Halve the cherry tomatoes | Rip the stems from the chilies or, if you prefer a spicy soup, keep the stems and split the chili down the middle to expose the seeds | Cut the ends off the green beans and slice them in half

Put the saucepan over medium heat | Pour in half the coconut milk and bring to a gentle simmer | Add the ginger, lemongrass, shallots, and lime leaves and stir very gently for 3–4 minutes | Pour in the remaining coconut milk and the water and simmer for 1 minute | Add the mushrooms and chilies and stir gently for 3–4 minutes

Add the green beans to the pan and stir gently for 1 minute | Add the bell pepper, cherry tomatoes, soy sauce, and coconut sugar and stir gently to mix everything together | Reduce the heat and leave to simmer for 7–8 minutes | Take the pan off the heat

To finish the soup | Rip the leaves from the cilantro and chop roughly | Halve and shred the scallions | Cut the limes in half and squeeze the juice into the soup | Stir two-thirds of the chopped cilantro leaves into the soup, reserving the rest, and simmer for 1 minute | Taste and add more soy sauce for saltiness or lime juice for sourness, if needed | Serve garnished with the reserved cilantro leaves and scallions

VIETNAMESE STICKY TOFU

This recipe is super-quick, packed full of flavor, and answers the age-old question, "what should I do with tofu?" It's a great dinner option if you don't have much time but want something absolutely delicious. Pressing the tofu is really important here as it needs to be the right, firm texture.

SERVES 2

1 (10 oz) block firm tofu (smoked tofu works well too)
1-inch piece fresh ginger
1 garlic clove
1 fresh red chili
4 scallions
2 tbsp lime juice (about 1½–2 limes)
6 tbsp cornstarch
vegetable oil, for frying
½ cup brown sugar
¼ cup soy sauce
⅔ cup coconut water
scant 2 cups cooked basmati rice, or use 1 (9 oz) bag microwavable rice, for serving
2 heads bok choy
2 tbsp sesame oil
¼ tsp salt
2 tsp sesame seeds

Tofu press or 2 clean tea towels and a weight such as a heavy book | Fine grater or Microplane | Large skillet | Line a plate with paper towels | Wok | Grill pan

....

Press the tofu using a tofu press or place it between two clean kitchen towels, lay it on a plate, and put a weight on top | Leave for at least 30 minutes to drain and firm up before you start cooking

Meanwhile, peel the ginger by scraping off the skin with a spoon and finely grate it | Peel and grate the garlic | Rip the stem from the chili, cut it in half lengthwise and remove the seeds if you prefer, then thinly slice | Finely chop two-thirds of the scallions | Ribbon the remaining scallions and keep to one side to garnish | Cut the limes in half

Put the cornstarch in a shallow bowl | Cut the drained tofu into 8 slices and roll them evenly in the cornstarch to coat

Place the skillet over medium-high heat | Pour enough vegetable oil into the pan to cover the bottom generously | Heat until a wooden spoon dipped into the oil sizzles around the edges | Lay the tofu in the pan and fry for 5–6 minutes, turning halfway | Drain on paper towels

Pour 1 tablespoon oil into the wok and place over high heat | Add the grated ginger and garlic, the chopped scallions, and the sliced chili | Stir-fry for 90 seconds | Sprinkle in the sugar and stir until a syrup forms | Stir in the soy sauce and coconut water | Bring to a rolling boil and cook for roughly 15 minutes, until the liquid has reduced by two-thirds | Squeeze in the lime juice | Reduce the heat to low

Heat the rice or cook it following the instructions on the package

To cook the bok choy, put the grill pan over high heat | Cut the bok choy into quarters | Put it in a mixing bowl and toss with the sesame oil and salt | Lay the bok choy on the hot grill pan, cut-side down, and cook until they get black char lines | Transfer to plates

Place the slices of prepared tofu in the wok, one by one, and toss carefully so they're well covered in the sticky sauce

Divide the rice between plates | Top with the sticky tofu | Drizzle over any leftover sauce | Garnish with reserved scallions and sesame seeds | Serve with the char-grilled bok choy

FAUX GRAS

This amazing recipe was the brainchild of Alexis Gauthier, and was shared with the world through a collaboration we did with him. Spread it on sourdough toast and serve with cornichons for the perfect starter or canapé with drinks—it tastes like proper, posh pâté! If you're eating it straightaway, serve in ramekins, or else store in sterilized jars in the fridge for up to a week.

MAKES 4 SMALL JARS OR RAMEKINS

2 sprigs fresh rosemary
3 sprigs fresh thyme
7 sage leaves
2 tbsp olive oil
1 large shallot
a pinch of salt
2 garlic cloves
18 button mushrooms
2 tbsp cognac
1¼ cups walnuts
2 cups cooked lentils (homemade or canned)
2½ tbsp soy sauce
½ or 1 very small cooked beet (about 1 oz)
3½ oz dairy-free butter
a few peppercorns, to garnish
good-quality toasted sourdough bread or baguette (or a pack of crackers), to serve
cornichons, to serve, optional

4 small sterilized glass jars or ramekins | Skillet | Food processor | Small saucepan

To sterilize the jars and lids, wash them in hot, soapy water then fill them to the top with boiling water | Drain on a kitchen towel until completely dry

Remove the leaves from the herbs by running your thumb and forefinger from the top to the base of the stems (the leaves should easily come away) | Reserve a few leaves and sprigs for garnish and finely chop the rest

Pour the oil into the skillet over medium heat | Peel and roughly chop the shallot and add it to the pan | Add a pinch of salt and cook for about 7 minutes, stirring occasionally, until translucent

Peel and roughly chop the garlic and add to the pan | Cook for 3 minutes longer | Chop the mushrooms and add them to the pan | Cook, stirring continuously, for 5 minutes, until everything is well softened | Add the finely chopped herbs and the cognac

Transfer the contents of the pan to the food processor | Chop the walnuts and add them to the processor with the cooked lentils, soy sauce, and beet | Blitz until almost smooth | Transfer the mixture to the prepared jars or ramekins and smooth the tops with the back of a spoon

Place the small saucepan over a low heat | Add the dairy-free butter and melt without heating it too much as it can split | Pour it over the pâté to completely cover | Place a few herb leaves and sprigs and peppercorns on top and leave to cool | Seal the jars (or cover the ramekins with plastic wrap) and refrigerate to chill

Serve with the toasted sourdough bread or crackers and cornichons, if using

GRILLED CHEESE SANDWICHES

We love how quick and satisfying a grilled cheese sandwich is! On the following pages are our three favorite fillings. We've also given you our recipe for dairy-free cheese. Tapioca flour helps the cheese firm up for optimum meltiness—you may need to go to a natural foods store to find it, but it'll be worth it (and you can use it in our mozzarella balls on page 102).

AMERICAN CLASSIC SANDWICH

MAKES 4

1½ oz pickles or cornichons
8 slices fresh sourdough bread
dairy-free butter, for spreading
Homemade Melty Cheese (see page 43)
2 tbsp yellow mustard
2 tbsp ketchup

Skillet

Thinly slice the pickles | Generously butter the bread with dairy-free butter | Put the skillet over medium heat

Place one slice of bread in the pan, buttered side down | Spread with a quarter of the cheese and lay the pickles on top | Dollop a quarter of the mustard and ketchup on top and spread them out | Place a slice of bread on top, buttered side up | Increase the heat to medium and press the bread down with a spatula until it starts to sizzle, 4–5 minutes

Flip the sandwich over and fry for another 4–5 minutes, until the bread is golden and crispy | Transfer to a cutting board, cut in half, and serve immediately | Repeat to make all the sandwiches

ENGLISH PLOUGHMAN'S SANDWICH

MAKES 4

8 slices fresh sourdough bread
dairy-free butter, for spreading
Homemade Melty Cheese (see opposite)
4 tbsp pickled chutney

Skillet over medium heat

....

Generously butter the bread with dairy-free butter

Place one slice of bread in the pan, buttered side down | Spread with a quarter of the cheese | Dollop 1 tablespoon of the chutney over the cheese and spread it around | Place a slice of bread on top, buttered side up | Increase the heat to medium and press the bread down with a spatula until it starts to sizzle, about 4−5 minutes

Flip the sandwich over and fry for another 4−5 minutes, until the bread is golden and crispy | Transfer to a cutting board, cut in half, and serve immediately | Repeat to make all the sandwiches

INDIAN-STYLE CHUTNEY SANDWICH

MAKES 4

1 scallion
8 slices fresh sourdough bread
dairy-free butter, for spreading
Homemade Melty Cheese (see opposite)
4 tbsp brinjal (eggplant) pickle

Skillet

....

Thinly slice the scallion | Generously butter the bread with dairy-free butter | Put the pan over medium heat

Place a slice of bread in the pan, buttered side down | Spread with a quarter of the cheese | Dollop 1 tablespoon of the brinjal pickle over the cheese | Sprinkle on a quarter of the scallion | Place a slice of bread on top, buttered side up | Increase the heat to medium and press the bread down with a spatula until it starts to sizzle, about 4−5 minutes

Flip the sandwich over and fry for another 4−5 minutes, until the bread is golden and crispy | Transfer to a cutting board, cut in half, and serve immediately | Repeat to make all the sandwiches

HOMEMADE MELTY CHEESE

This cheese has a delicious gooey consistency, particularly when melted, making it perfect for grilled cheese sandwiches. The recipe makes more than you need for the sandwiches so keep the leftovers in the fridge for a couple of days.

MAKES 9–10 oz

2 oz cashews
1 carrot (about 2½ oz)
2 cups + 2 tbsp water
1 small garlic clove
⅔ cup aquafaba (the drained water from
    1–2 [15 oz] cans chickpeas)
2 tbsp tapioca flour
1 tbsp coconut oil
½ tsp salt, plus more to taste
2 tbsp nutritional yeast
¼ lemon
black pepper, to taste

Small saucepan | Blender

First cook the cashews and carrot | Peel and finely chop the carrot | Put the cashews in the saucepan with the carrot and cover them with the water | Put the pan over high heat, bring to a boil, and cook for 20 minutes | Take off the heat, save 1¼ cups of the cooking liquid, then drain the cashews and carrot | Peel the garlic

Now combine all the ingredients together | Put the cashews, carrot, garlic, aquafaba, tapioca flour, coconut oil, salt, nutritional yeast, and the reserved cooking liquid into the blender | Squeeze in the lemon juice, catching any seeds in your other hand | Blend until you have a smooth cream

Pour the cream back into the saucepan, taste, and season with salt and pepper | Put the pan over medium heat and cook, stirring constantly, for 5–6 minutes, until the cheese has a thick, homogenous texture | Pour into a bowl, cover, leave to cool, then refrigerate until needed

SINGAPORE FRIED VERMICELLI

Quick, satisfying, and spicy, this is perhaps our favorite ever noodle dish. It is the perfect accompaniment to an Asian feast. Try it with our Vietnamese Sticky Tofu (see page 36) or Speedy Hoisin Mushrooms (see page 64). Feel free to freestyle on the veg—this is a great fridge-raid recipe.

SERVES 4–6

4 garlic cloves
5 oz fresh mushrooms
4 scallions
3 fresh red chilies
3½ oz broccolini
1 head bok choy (about 3½ oz)
1 large carrot
1 red bell pepper
8 oz dried rice vermicelli
¼ cup vegetable oil
4½ tbsp soy sauce
2 tsp curry powder
1 tbsp sugar
2 tbsp water
a pinch of salt
a pinch of black pepper
1 lime

Boiling water | Fine grater or Microplane | Wok

Get all the veggies ready to stir-fry | Peel and grate the garlic | Thinly slice the mushrooms and scallions | Rip the stems from two of the chilies, cut them in half lengthwise, removing the seeds if you prefer less heat, then finely chop | Chop the broccolini into ¾-inch pieces | Trim the bok choy and separate the leaves | Peel the carrot and then use the peeler to slice long, thin ribbons | Cut the bell pepper in half and cut out the stem and seeds, then slice into thin strips

Prepare the vermicelli following the instructions on the package | Keep checking them as you want the noodles to still be a little firm when you add them to the wok, as they will carry on cooking

Put the wok over high heat and add the oil | Once the pan is really hot, add the garlic, chopped chilies, and mushrooms | Stir-fry for 30 seconds, then add the rest of the veg | Stir in the soy sauce, curry powder, and sugar and stir-fry for 2 minutes longer | Drain the noodles and stir them into the veggies | Add the water

Season with the salt and pepper | Cut the lime in half and squeeze in the juice, to taste | Rip the stem from the remaining chili, thinly slice, and scatter over the top

GUACAJACKS

Ian came up with the name for this and now the Guacajack shall live on forever as an incredibly easy, delicious meal that we make all the time. We've given traditional guac a special BOSH! treatment with added black beans for extra bite and a bonus protein boost, with chopped cherry tomatoes and shallots for freshness.

SERVES 2

2 large sweet potatoes
2 tbsp chili oil (store-bought or make our
    Homemade Chili Oil, see below)
salt

FOR THE BLACK BEAN GUACAMOLE
2 small ripe avocados
1 large shallot
½ garlic clove
1 small fresh red chili
6 cherry tomatoes
1 lime
½ oz cilantro
half (14 oz) can black beans
1 tbsp olive oil, optional

Preheat oven to 350°F | Line a sheet pan with parchment paper | Fine grater or Microplane

Put the sweet potatoes on the sheet pan and pierce them a few times with a fork | Rub the potatoes with the chili oil and a generous pinch of salt | Put the pan in the oven and bake for 50–55 minutes, until the skin has begun to crisp up and the flesh is tender

When the potatoes are nearly cooked, make your guac | Halve and carefully pit the avocados by tapping the pit firmly with the heel of a knife so that it lodges in the stone, then twist and remove | Spoon the flesh into a mixing bowl and mash with a fork | Peel and finely chop the shallot | Peel and grate the garlic | Rip the stem from the chili, cut it in half lengthwise, and remove the seeds, then finely chop | Finely chop the cherry tomatoes | Add the shallots, garlic, chili, and tomatoes to the bowl | Halve the lime and squeeze in the juice | Fold everything together to combine | Taste and season with salt | Pick the leaves from the cilantro and discard the stems | Set aside a third of the leaves for garnish, then finely chop the rest and add to the bowl | Drain and rinse the black beans and stir them into the guacamole | If the consistency is a little stiff, add a little olive oil to soften it

Take the pan out of the oven and leave the potatoes to cool for 5 minutes | Carefully slice open the sweet potatoes and gently fluff the flesh with a fork | Spoon half the guacamole into each potato | Garnish with the reserved cilantro leaves and serve immediately

HOMEMADE CHILI OIL

MAKES 1 cup

1 cup + 2 tbsp light olive oil
4 dried ancho chilies
1 tbsp red pepper flakes

Sterilized bottle or jar (see page 39) | Saucepan

Pour the 2 tablespoons oil into a pan and heat | Add the chilies and pepper flakes and stir for 1 minute | Pour in the rest of the oil, turn the heat right down, and warm through for about 5 minutes, being careful not to let the oil bubble | Take off the heat and cool to room temperature | Pour into the bottle or jar and screw on the lid | Use within 1 month

QUICK QUESADILLAS

There's nothing like a little Mexican food to get the day moving along just right! Use whole-grain wheat or corn tortillas if you are cutting down on processed wheat flour. These are also great served with a simple tomato salad.

SERVES 4

1 red onion
1 garlic clove
2 large roasted red peppers from a jar
3½ oz dairy-free cheese
1 large avocado
1 oz cilantro
1 lime
1 (14 oz) can black beans (or kidney beans)
2 tbsp + 1 tsp olive oil
1 (14.5 oz) can diced tomatoes
1 tsp cayenne pepper, plus a little more
¾ cup corn kernels
4 large flour tortillas
salt and black pepper

Fine grater or Microplane | 2 large skillets

First get all your ingredients ready | Peel and thinly slice the red onion | Peel and grate the garlic | Cut the roasted red peppers into strips | Grate the dairy-free cheese | Halve and carefully stone the avocado by tapping the pit firmly with the heel of a knife so that it lodges in the pit, then twist and remove | Scoop out the flesh and cut into small chunks | Pick the leaves from the cilantro and chop finely | Cut the lime in half | Drain and rinse the beans

Place a skillet over medium heat | Add 2 tablespoons olive oil | Add the onion to the hot pan with a pinch of salt and sweat for 7–8 minutes, until softened | Add the garlic and stir for 1–2 minutes | Add the roasted red pepper strips, black beans, tomatoes, and 1 teaspoon cayenne pepper and cook for 5 minutes | Remove from the heat and stir in the corn | Taste and season with salt and pepper | Add more cayenne if you want more heat | Squeeze over the lime juice

Put the second skillet over medium heat | Add 1 teaspoon oil | Lay a tortilla in the pan and sprinkle on a generous handful of grated cheese | Spoon a quarter of the filling onto the tortilla and spread it over one half | Sprinkle avocado and cilantro on top of the filling

Once the cheese has melted, check the underside of the tortilla—if golden cooking spots are appearing, the quesadilla is ready | Use a spatula to fold it in half, sandwiching the filling | Remove from the pan, slice into wedges, and serve immediately | Repeat to make all the quesadillas

BANGIN' BURGERS

Here are a couple of bangin' quick burgers, inspired by our travels to Ibiza, for Addison's bachelor party, and LA. The brilliant balsamic onions and classic burger sauce are great with everything BBQ and the hash browns in the LA burger add an amazing extra layer of flavor and texture. Customize your burger; just be sure to migrate beyond ketchup and lettuce!

IBIZA SUNSET BURGER

SERVES 2

2 plant-based burger patties, or
    The Big BOSH! Burgers from our
    first book, *BOSH!*, page 119
2 slices dairy-free cheese
2 gherkin pickles
1 little gem lettuce
2 good-quality burger buns

FOR THE BALSAMIC ONIONS
1 large red onion
1 tbsp olive oil
2 tsp brown sugar
2 tsp balsamic vinegar

FOR THE BOSH! BURGER SAUCE
3½ tbsp egg-free mayonnaise
1 tbsp gherkin brine (from the jar)
½ tsp maple syrup
¼ tsp vinegar
¼ tsp white pepper
½ tsp Dijon mustard
¼ tsp onion powder
¼ tsp garlic powder
¼ tsp smoked paprika

Preheat oven to 350°F | Line a sheet pan | Skillet over a low heat | Roasting pan

....

First make the Balsamic Onions | Peel and thinly slice the red onion | Add the olive oil to the skillet over low heat | Add the onion and fry for 12–15 minutes, stirring occasionally, until lightly browned | Add the sugar and balsamic vinegar and stir for 3–4 minutes, until the sugar has dissolved and the onions have darkened | Take the pan off the heat

Put the burger patties on the lined sheet pan | Put the pan in the oven and cook following the instructions on the package | 5 minutes before they're ready, lay a slice of dairy-free cheese on top of each patty and place an upturned roasting pan over the patties to stop the cheese drying out | Bake for the remaining 5 minutes

Meanwhile, make the BOSH! Burger Sauce by combining all the ingredients in a small bowl and mixing together with a fork

Slice the gherkins | Shred the lettuce

Assemble your burgers! Slice the burger buns in half and spread the bottoms with the BOSH! Burger Sauce | Take the burgers and cheese out of the oven and place one patty on each burger bun | Top the cheese with the shredded lettuce and sliced gherkins and then pile on the balsamic onions | Close the lids of the burgers and serve

LA GUACBURGER

SERVES 2

2 plant-based burger patties, or
   The Big BOSH! Burgers from our
   first book, *BOSH!*, page 119
4 slices dairy-free cheese
2 good-quality burger buns
2 tbsp egg-free mayonnaise
4 little gem lettuce leaves
1 large tomato

FOR THE GUACAMOLE
1 lime
1 small garlic clove
¼ tsp salt
1 large ripe avocado
1 small fresh red chili
2 scallions
4 cherry tomatoes
½ oz cilantro

FOR THE HASH BROWNS
1 large potato
2 tbsp all-purpose flour
¾ tsp salt
¼ tsp black pepper
olive oil, for shallow frying

Preheat oven to 350°F | Fine grater or Microplane | Clean kitchen towel | Skillet | Line a plate with paper towels | Line a sheet pan | Roasting pan

First make the guacamole | Halve the lime and squeeze the juice into a bowl | Peel and grate the garlic into the bowl | Add the salt | Halve and carefully pit the avocado by tapping the pit firmly with the heel of a knife so that it lodges in the pit, then twist and remove | Scoop the flesh into the bowl | Use the back of a fork to mash everything together

Rip the stem from the chili, cut it in half lengthwise, remove the seeds, and finely chop | Trim and finely chop the scallions and cherry tomatoes and add them to the bowl | Pick the leaves from the cilantro, roughly chop, and add them to the bowl | Stir all the ingredients together with a fork so they're well mixed | Taste and add a little more seasoning if necessary | Cover and refrigerate

Peel the potato for the Hash Browns and grate it into a sieve | Wash under cold water until the water runs clear | Tip into the clean kitchen towel and twist the towel over the sink to squeeze out all the excess moisture | Put the grated potato into a mixing bowl | Sprinkle in the flour, salt, and pepper and mix everything together | Roll the grated potato into 2 balls and squash them into ⅓-inch-thick patties

Put the skillet over medium heat | Pour in the olive oil until it's ⅓ inch deep | Warm until a wooden spoon dipped into the oil sizzles around the edges | Carefully place the hash browns in the oil and cook for 3–4 minutes on each side, until golden brown and crispy | Transfer to the plate lined with paper towels to drain

Put the burger patties on the lined sheet pan | Put the pan in the oven and cook following the instructions on the package | 5 minutes before they're ready, lay a slice of dairy-free cheese and a hash brown on top of each patty and place an upturned roasting pan over the patties to stop the cheese drying out | Bake for the remaining 5 minutes

To assemble the burgers, slice the buns in half and spread the bottoms with the egg-free mayo | Cover with 2 lettuce leaves for each bun | Cut the tomato into thick slices and lay them over the lettuce | Take the burgers, cheese, and hash browns out of the oven and place one patty on each bun | Dollop the guacamole over the tops | Close the lids of the burgers and serve

Pictured on pages 52–53

LA GUACBURGER

IBIZA SUNSET
BURGER

LA GUACBURGER

BROCCAULIFLOWER CHEESE

An easy, punchy, gorgeously warming dish that is perfect for a winter evening. As it's packed with veggies and low on processed carbs it's also not too heavy. Feel free to roast any veggies you like to add to this bake. The roux used in this dish is really reliable and would work well in any creamy pasta bake.

SERVES 4

1 head cauliflower (about 1 lb 5 oz)
1 head broccoli (about 12 oz)
1½ tbsp olive oil
3½ oz fresh spinach leaves
½ cup panko breadcrumbs
fresh chives, for garnish, optional
7 oz salad greens, for serving
salt and black pepper

FOR THE CHEESY SAUCE
3½ tbsp dairy-free butter
6 tbsp all-purpose flour
3 cups unsweetened plant-based milk
7 oz dairy-free cheese
5 tbsp nutritional yeast
1 oz pickled jalapeños
1½ tsp garlic powder
¾ tsp smoked paprika
2½ tsp English mustard

Preheat oven to 350°F | Line a sheet pan | Large saucepan over medium heat | Whisk | Grater | 8 x 12-inch baking dish

Trim the cauliflower and broccoli and cut into small florets | Cut the stems into similar-sized pieces | Spread over the lined sheet pan | Sprinkle with a little salt and pepper and 1 tablespoon olive oil | Put the pan in the oven and bake for 20–25 minutes

Meanwhile, make the cheesy sauce | Put the dairy-free butter into the medium-hot saucepan and stir with a wooden spoon until it melts, then gradually add the flour to the pan, stirring vigorously until you have a doughy paste | Gradually pour in 2 cups of the milk, whisking all the time until you have a thick, creamy sauce

Grate the dairy-free cheese | Add the cheese, nutritional yeast, jalapeños, garlic powder, paprika, and mustard to the pan, stirring constantly, until the cheese has melted and combined with the sauce | Add the rest of the milk and keep stirring until the sauce has a thick, creamy consistency | Taste, season to perfection with salt and pepper, and turn the heat down

Take the pan out of the oven and turn on the broiler to high | Add the cauliflower and broccoli to the pan of cheese sauce | Add the spinach and fold so that everything is well covered in sauce | Pour into the baking dish and smooth out with the back of a wooden spoon

Pour the panko breadcrumbs into a dish and drizzle over the remaining ½ tablespoon olive oil | Toss to coat | Sprinkle the breadcrumbs over the top of the cheesy vegetables

Put the baking dish under the broiler until golden, 1–5 minutes depending on your broiler, so watch it closely | Remove the dish from the oven | Spoon into bowls | Snip over the chives to garnish, if using, and serve with the salad greens on the side

EGGPLANT KATSU

We've been refining this dish for some time now to achieve the perfect balance of a beautifully light but comfortingly warm katsu sauce. Katsu is amazing with the mighty eggplant. You can also make double the sauce and freeze half; it will keep for a month (defrost it overnight in the fridge before reheating).

SERVES 4

1⅓ cups all-purpose flour
½ tbsp salt
1 cup unsweetened plant-based milk
1⅓ cups panko breadcrumbs
2 eggplants (about 10 oz each)
4 cups cooked basmati rice, or use
    2 (9 oz) bags microwavable
    basmati rice, for serving
4 scallions
white sesame seeds, for sprinkling
vegetable oil, for frying

FOR THE KATSU SAUCE
1 large onion
1 small carrot
2-inch piece fresh ginger
2 garlic cloves
2 tbsp sesame oil
1 tbsp olive oil
1½ tsp soy sauce
1 tbsp curry powder
1½ cups vegetable stock
1 lemon
salt
2 tsp garam masala
1 tsp sugar
1 tbsp cornstarch
2 tbsp water

Fine grater or Microplane | 2 large skillets | Blender | Whisk | Line a large plate with paper towels

First make the sauce | Peel and dice the onion | Peel and grate the carrot | Peel the ginger by scraping off the skin with a spoon, then finely grate | Peel and grate the garlic

Put one skillet over medium heat and warm the sesame oil | Add the onion and fry for 3–4 minutes, stirring | Add the carrot and olive oil and stir for 5–6 minutes | Add the garlic and ginger and stir for 2 minutes | Add the soy sauce and curry powder and stir for 2 minutes, then transfer to the blender along with the vegetable stock | Blend | Pour back into the pan and return to medium heat

Cut the lemon in half and squeeze the juice of half into the same pan, catching any seeds with your other hand | Sprinkle with the garam masala and sugar and stir | Reduce the heat to low | Taste and add salt and more lemon if required | Put the cornstarch and water into a small dish and mix together with a fork | Pour into the pan and stir to thicken

Now make the batter | Put the flour, salt, and milk into a mixing bowl and whisk to a smooth batter | Tip the breadcrumbs into a separate bowl

Trim the eggplants and cut into ⅓-inch-thick slices | Tip them into the batter and toss to coat | Pick out one slice and roll it around in the breadcrumbs, covering it completely | Repeat to coat all the slices

Fry the eggplant | Pour the vegetable oil into the second skillet until it's ¾ inch deep | Put the pan over medium heat and heat until a wooden spoon dipped into the oil starts to bubble around the edges | Carefully add the eggplant slices and fry in batches for 3–4 minutes on each side, until crispy and deep golden | Transfer to the paper towels for a minute to soak up any excess oil

Meanwhile, heat the rice, if necessary, or cook following the instructions on the package, then divide among plates | Arrange the crispy eggplant on top and drizzle over the katsu sauce | Thinly slice the scallions and sprinkle them with the sesame seeds before serving

GREEK GYROS

Tzatziki is a wonderful dip for things like nachos and crudités or simply spread over bread, so make an extra batch of it to use in another meal. You can make these mushrooms a day ahead and reheat them. If you don't fancy bread, this would make a really great salad box.

SERVES 4

2 red onions
2 garlic cloves
14 oz shiitake mushrooms
3 tbsp olive oil
2 tbsp red wine vinegar
2 tsp dried oregano
1 tsp dried thyme
1 tsp dried rosemary
½ tsp smoked paprika
½ tsp sugar
1 tsp salt
1 large tomato
½ head little gem lettuce
4 pita breads (roughly 8 inches
   in diameter)

FOR THE TZATZIKI
½ cucumber
1½ tbsp salt
1 lemon
1 small garlic clove
4 fresh mint leaves
½ oz fresh dill
7 oz Greek-style coconut yogurt
a drizzle of olive oil
salt and black pepper

Fine grater or Microplane | 2 skillets | Clean kitchen towel | Cut out four 9-inch squares of parchment paper

First make the tzatziki | Peel the cucumber and grate it into a bowl | Sprinkle with the salt and stir to coat | Set aside for 15 minutes

Peel and thinly slice the onions for your gyros | Peel and grate the garlic | Cut the mushrooms into ⅓-inch-thick strips

Put a skillet over medium heat and pour in 2 tablespoons olive oil | Add half the sliced onion and fry for 3–4 minutes | Add the garlic and stir for 2 minutes | Add the remaining olive oil | Tip in the mushrooms and stir them into the onions for 3–4 minutes | Add the red wine vinegar, oregano, thyme, rosemary, paprika, sugar, and salt | Fold everything together and cook for 7–8 minutes | Reduce the heat to low and keep warm, stirring occasionally

To finish the tzatziki, tip the cucumber into the middle of a clean kitchen towel, gather up the edges, and squeeze out the excess water | Put the strained cucumber back into the bowl | Cut the lemon in half and squeeze in the juice of one half, catching any seeds in your other hand | Peel the garlic and finely grate it into the bowl | Finely chop the mint leaves and dill and add them to the bowl | Pour in the coconut yogurt and mix everything together with a spoon | Taste and season with more lemon juice, if necessary, salt, pepper and a drizzle of olive oil

Thinly slice the tomato | Shred the lettuce

Warm the pita breads | Put the second skillet over medium heat | Gently warm the pitas in the pan for a minute on each side

Lay the squares of parchment paper on a clean surface and put a pita on each one | Spread with a generous helping of tzatziki | Top with the lettuce, tomato slices, an equal serving of the mushroom mixture, and the rest of the sliced onion | Wrap your gyros up in the parchment paper and serve immediately

PIRI PIRI CHORIZO BAKE

This is a quick and easy-to-throw-together, eat-the-rainbow revelation. Colored heirloom tomatoes are a great addition if you can get hold of them. The piri piri sauce is wonderful, so consider making double and keeping half for another recipe. Serve with brown rice for an even healthier meal.

SERVES 4

2 medium sweet potatoes
olive oil
1 lemon
1 red bell pepper
1 green bell pepper
1 yellow bell pepper
3 garlic cloves
10 oz Eazy Chorizo (see opposite) or
    shop-bought veggie chorizo sausages
20 cherry tomatoes
4 cups cooked basmati rice, or use
    2 (9 oz) bags microwavable
    basmati rice, to serve
¾ oz cilantro
salt and black pepper

FOR THE PIRI PIRI SAUCE
1 red onion
4 garlic cloves
1 red bell pepper
2 fresh red chilies (Scotch bonnet,
    red, or bird's-eye)
2 tbsp smoked paprika
1 tsp dried oregano
2 tbsp red wine vinegar
a large bunch of fresh basil
1 lemon

Preheat oven to 350°F | Large microwavable bowl, optional | Roasting pan | Blender | Fine grater or Microplane

First cook the sweet potatoes | Peel the sweet potatoes and cut them into ¾-inch cubes | Put them in a large microwavable bowl, sprinkle with a pinch of salt and pepper, and drizzle with olive oil | Cut the lemon in half and squeeze over the juice, catching any seeds in your other hand | Toss to coat | Cover the bowl with a plate and microwave on high for 6 minutes, until soft | Alternatively, cook in the oven at 350°F for 30–35 minutes, until soft

Cut the bell peppers in half, cut out the stems and seeds, and cut the flesh into ¾-inch cubes, then put them in the roasting pan | Use the back of a knife to lightly crush the 3 garlic cloves and add them to the pan | Drizzle with a little olive oil and sprinkle with salt and pepper | Add the sweet potatoes to the peppers and put the pan in the oven for 10–15 minutes, until the peppers have small black patches on the skins

Meanwhile, make the Eazy Chorizo sausages following the recipe opposite (or cut up store-bought sausages into bite-sized pieces and cook following the instructions on the package)

To make the piri piri sauce, peel and roughly chop the onion and garlic | Cut the bell pepper in half and cut out the stem and seeds | Rip the stems from the chilies, cut them in half lengthwise, and remove the seeds if you prefer a milder sauce | Put the onion, garlic, pepper, and chilies in the blender with the paprika, oregano, red wine vinegar, and basil | Grate in the zest of the lemon, then cut it in half and squeeze in the juice, catching any seeds | Add a drop of water and blend to a smooth paste | Taste and adjust the seasoning, if necessary

Remove the roasting pan from the oven | Transfer the sausages and piri piri sauce to the pan and mix everything together | Add the cherry tomatoes and put the pan back in the oven for 15 minutes, until the potatoes and peppers are cooked and the sauce is piping hot

Heat the rice or cook it following the instructions on the package

Pluck the leaves from the cilantro and discard the stems | Coarsely chop the leaves and sprinkle them over the vegetables | Serve with rice

Pictured on pages 62–63

EAZY CHORIZO

Once we'd developed this quick DIY chorizo recipe we never looked back. Hitting a standard store-bought veggie sausage with fennel, paprika, red wine, and maple syrup gives an instant chorizo vibe.

MAKES 10 oz

10 oz plant-based sausages
2 tbsp olive oil
1½ tsp smoked paprika
½ tsp cayenne pepper
¼ tsp ground fennel
a pinch of salt
a pinch of black pepper
2 garlic cloves
¼ cup red wine
½ tbsp maple syrup

Medium skillet over medium-high heat | Fine grater or Microplane

Slice the sausages into ¾-inch-thick rounds | Put them in the hot pan and pour in the olive oil | Fry for 5 minutes, turning them now and again, until golden | Sprinkle with the paprika, cayenne pepper, fennel, salt, and pepper | Peel and finely grate the garlic into the pan and fry for another 2 minutes

Carefully add the red wine and maple syrup to the pan and cook until the wine has reduced and you have a sticky glaze, stirring occasionally | Toss to ensure the sausage is covered | Take off the heat once all the liquid in the pan has evaporated, and serve

SPEEDY HOISIN MUSHROOMS

Did you know "hoisin" means "seafood"? And yet it neither contains seafood nor is traditionally served with seafood. Either way, we love it. From our first experiences of crispy pancakes to wonderful hoisin stir-fries, it remains a firm favorite. Try subbing little gem lettuce for the bok choy or pair with brown rice and greens for a healthy lunchbox.

SERVES 4

2 garlic cloves
1½-inch piece fresh ginger
½ oz cilantro
6 scallions
1 lb mixed mushrooms
2 heads bok choy
3 tbsp sesame oil
1 tbsp canola oil
1½ tbsp soy sauce
2½ tbsp hoisin sauce
1 tbsp sriracha
4 cups cooked basmati rice,
    or use 2 (9 oz) bags microwavable
    basmati rice, for serving
4 tsp white sesame seeds

Fine grater or Microplane | Wok | Grill pan

Peel and grate the garlic into a small bowl | Peel the ginger by scraping off the skin with a spoon, then grate into the bowl

Separate the cilantro leaves and stems and thinly slice both | Thinly slice the scallions | Roughly chop the mushrooms into bite-sized pieces

Cut the bok choy lengthwise into quarters, put them in a mixing bowl, and toss with 2 tablespoons of the sesame oil

Add the remaining 1 tablespoon of sesame oil and the canola oil to the wok and set over medium heat | When the oil is hot, add three-quarters of the scallions, the garlic, ginger, and chopped cilantro stems | Fry for 2 minutes, stirring constantly | Add the mushrooms and continue to stir for 6–7 minutes | Add the soy, hoisin, and sriracha sauces and stir for 1 minute, making sure the mushrooms are well coated | Turn the heat down while you cook your bok choy

Put the grill pan over high heat | While the pan is heating up, heat the rice, if necessary, or cook following the instructions on the package

Lay the bok choy on the grill pan and cook until char lines appear, trying not to move them around too much | Turn and cook the other sides

Divide the rice among bowls | Nestle the bok choy alongside | Spoon over the hoisin mushrooms | Sprinkle over the remaining scallions, cilantro leaves, and sesame seeds and serve

2

Henry's favorite
Curry House Jalfrezi

Ian's favorite
Shepherd's Pie

BÚN BÒ HUÉ

After traveling around Southeast Asia this dish became Henry's firm favorite. It's a fiery broth, but there's something about this soup that allows you to handle much more heat than you would expect! Double up the broth if you have a pan big enough and freeze half, ready to defrost when you are ready for a really quick soup.

SERVES 4

4 fresh bird's-eye or finger chilies
1 lime
2 scallions
7 oz mixed mushrooms
7 oz glass noodles
7 oz bean sprouts
4 heads baby bok choy
1 oz fresh mint
1 oz cilantro
1 oz Thai basil

FOR THE BROTH
1 onion
1 lemongrass stalk
3-inch piece fresh ginger
6 garlic cloves
3½ oz pineapple (fresh or canned)
1 green apple
1 fresh red chili (we prefer bird's-eye or finger chilies, but be warned that they're hot!)
¼ oz dried shiitake mushrooms (or use dried porcini)
5 kaffir lime leaves
2 star anise
3 tbsp coconut sugar
4¼ cups cold water
⅔ cup soy sauce
salt and black pepper

FOR THE HOT SAUCE
1 long lemongrass stalk
2 large shallots
2 garlic cloves
2 tbsp + 1 tsp canola oil
½ tbsp chili flakes
½ tbsp chili powder
1 tbsp soy sauce
2 tbsp water
1 tsp maple syrup

1 large stockpot | Fine grater or Microplane | Small skillet

First make the broth | Peel and halve the onion | Chop the lemongrass in half and lightly bash it with the base of a knife to release the oils | Peel the ginger by scraping off the skin with a spoon and slice | Peel and slice the garlic | Chop the pineapple into chunks | Peel and core the apple and chop roughly | Slice the chili lengthwise | Put all the broth ingredients into the stockpot over medium-high heat | Bring to the boil and simmer briskly until half the liquid has evaporated | Use a slotted spoon or sieve to remove all the solid ingredients and discard | Taste, season with salt and pepper, and set aside

To make the hot sauce, peel and discard the hard outer bark of the lemongrass and thinly slice | Peel and mince the shallots | Peel and finely grate the garlic | Pour the canola oil into the skillet and place it over medium-low heat | Add the sliced lemongrass to the pan and stir for 2 minutes | Add the shallots and stir for 2 minutes | Add the garlic and stir for 1 minute | Add the chili flakes and chili powder and stir for 1 minute | Add the soy sauce, water, and maple syrup and fry for 1 minute | Reduce the heat to a gentle simmer and cook for 3–5 minutes to reduce and thicken | Take off the heat

Prepare the garnishes | Thinly slice the chilies | Quarter the lime | Trim and thinly slice the scallions | Chop the mushrooms into bite-sized pieces

Put the broth back on the heat and bring to a boil, then reduce to a gentle simmer | Add the mushrooms and cook for 4 minutes | Add the noodles and cook in the broth following the instructions on the package

Divide the mushrooms and noodles among bowls | Add 2 teaspoons of the hot sauce to each bowl | Ladle in the broth | Add the bean sprouts, bok choy, mint, cilantro, and Thai basil leaves | Garnish with the chopped chilies, scallions, and lime wedges | Serve immediately

IAN'S DELIGHTFUL DAAL & ROTI

This is a certified hug-in-a-bowl, and is perhaps one of the finest flavor symphonies we've created. The spice blend is simple but perfectly balanced, and complements the rest of the ingredients. The daal tastes just as good the day after, reheated to piping hot, and the rotis will keep on a plate wrapped in plastic wrap for a couple of days, so definitely make more than you need!

SERVES 4

1 large onion
1 oz cilantro
3 garlic cloves
1-inch piece fresh ginger
2½ tbsp olive oil
½ tsp salt
1 tsp chili flakes
½ tbsp ground cumin
1 tsp ground turmeric
4 tsp garam masala
1 tsp superfine sugar
1 tsp ground coriander
1 tsp ground fenugreek
7 oz dried red lentils
1 (14.5 oz) can diced tomatoes
2 cups vegetable stock
1 (13.5 oz) can full-fat coconut milk
5 tbsp boiling water, optional

FOR THE ROTI

1⅔ cups self-rising flour, plus extra
    for dusting
½ tsp salt
1 tbsp vegetable oil
7 tbsp water
vegetable oil, for frying

Brush some plastic wrap with oil | Fine grater or Microplane | Large saucepan | Skillet | Rolling pin or clean, dry wine bottle

....

Start by making the roti | Pour the flour, salt, and oil into a large mixing bowl | Make a small well in the center and pour in the water | Use your hands to mix the ingredients together and knead until it comes together in a smooth ball of dough | Cover the bowl with the oiled plastic wrap and set it aside to rest for 20 minutes

Meanwhile, peel and finely chop the onion | Rip the leaves from the cilantro | Finely chop the stems and roughly chop the leaves | Peel and finely grate the garlic | Peel the ginger by scraping off the skin with a spoon and grate finely

Pour the olive oil into the saucepan and warm it over medium heat | Add the chopped onion and salt and stir for 5–7 minutes, until softened | Add the garlic, ginger, red pepper flakes, and cilantro stems to the pan and stir for 2–3 minutes | Add the cumin, turmeric, garam masala, sugar, ground coriander, and fenugreek and stir together for 30 seconds

Rinse the lentils and tip them into the pan | Stir for 1 minute | Pour in the diced tomatoes, fold them into the lentils, and bring the thick sauce to a gentle simmer | Pour in the vegetable stock and coconut milk and stir all the ingredients together until well mixed | Bring back to a very gentle simmer, put the lid on the pan, and leave it to bubble away for 35–40 minutes until thickened, stirring every now and then to make sure the daal doesn't catch on the bottom of the pan

While the daal is cooking, return to the roti | Take the dough out of the bowl and divide it into 8 equal pieces | Place the pieces of dough on a cutting board and cover with the oiled plastic wrap | Dust a clean surface with flour, take a piece of dough, and roll it out into a neat, flat circle, as thin as you can get it | Repeat with the remaining pieces

Put the skillet over high heat until very hot | Pour 1 teaspoon oil into the pan and swish it around to coat the base | Place a roti in the pan and cook until it starts to bubble, then flip it over and fry the other side for another minute | Transfer to a plate and repeat to cook all the roti

Once your daal is cooked, take the lid off the pan, taste it, and season as necessary | If the lentils have too much bite, stir in 5 tbsp boiling water, put the lid back on, and simmer for 3–5 minutes longer | Stir in the roughly chopped cilantro leaves and serve immediately with the roti

Pictured on pages 72–73

CURRY HOUSE JALFREZI

The spicy and flavorful jalfrezi has now overtaken tikka masala as Britain's favorite curry! This stock can be prepared in advance and frozen or kept in the fridge in an airtight container, so make a double batch to save time. Be sure to taste the curry as you go to get the perfect balance, as spices can vary in strength.

SERVES 3–4

1 large eggplant
¼ cup sunflower or olive oil
1 onion
1 red bell pepper
a small bunch of cilantro
5 green bird's-eye chilies
12 cherry tomatoes
3 tbsp curry powder
1 tsp garam masala
¼–2 tsp hot chili powder
½ cup tomato paste
4 cups cooked basmati rice, or use
     2 (9 oz) bags microwavable
     basmati rice, for serving
salt

FOR THE STOCK
1 onion
2-inch piece fresh ginger
5 garlic cloves
2 cups + 1 tbsp water
½ fresh red chili
3 cherry tomatoes
1 tbsp sunflower or olive oil
¼ tsp ground coriander
¼ tsp ground cumin
¼ tsp ground fenugreek
¼ tsp ground turmeric
¼ tsp paprika

Preheat the broiler to high | Sheet pan | Fine grater or Microplane | Medium saucepan | Blender

First cook the eggplant | Trim the eggplant and cut it into ¾-inch chunks | Spread over the sheet pan | Sprinkle with 2 tablespoons oil and a good pinch of salt | Toss to coat | Broil for 15 minutes, turning occasionally | Remove when golden brown all over but not burnt

Meanwhile, make the stock | Peel and finely chop the onion | Peel the ginger by scraping off the skin with a spoon and grate | Peel and grate the garlic | Put the ginger and garlic into a bowl and mix with 1 tablespoon water to make a paste

Finely chop the red chili and tomatoes | Place the saucepan over medium heat and pour in the oil | Add the onion and sauté for 5 minutes | Add a teaspoon of the ginger and garlic paste | Add all the remaining spices and half the water and stir | Simmer for 10 minutes, until browned and reduced completely | Pour in the rest of the water, stir, and transfer to the blender | Blend to a smooth liquid | Clean out the pan

Back to the curry | Peel and thinly slice the onion | Cut the bell pepper in half and cut out the stem and seeds, then thinly slice | Pick the leaves from the cilantro | Finely chop the stems and roughly chop the leaves | Trim and thinly slice two of the chilies | Quarter the tomatoes

Pour the remaining oil into the clean saucepan | Place over high heat | Add the onion, bell pepper, and sliced chilies and fry for 3 minutes, stirring regularly | Stir in the chopped cilantro stems and remaining ginger and garlic paste (from making the stock) | Add the curry powder, garam masala, ¼ teaspoon hot chili powder, tomato paste, broiled eggplant, and stock | Taste and add more salt, garam masala, and chili powder if needed | Stir in the tomatoes | Simmer gently for 10 minutes, stirring frequently, until slightly thickened

Heat the rice or cook it following the instructions on the package

Transfer to a serving dish | Cut the remaining chilies in half lengthwise and use them to garnish the curry along with the chopped cilantro leaves | Serve with the rice

ULTIMATE FALAFEL WRAP

Falafel has come to the rescue for us many times on a night out when we're a bit peckish, so we decided to re-create our own ultimate wrap for you guys to make at home. We recommend making your own hummus and chili jam but if you're feeling a bit lazy, feel free to use store-bought ones instead.

SERVES 4

5 oz Chili Jam (see page 79, or use
    5 oz store-bought)
Falafel (see page 78)
Hummus (see page 196, or use
    14 oz store-bought)
Flatbreads (see page 78, or use
    4 store-bought)
¼ cup fresh baby spinach or field greens
onion pickle, for serving (see page 107
    or use any store-bought pickle relish)
flat-leaf parsley, to garnish

Food processor | Large saucepan | Sterilized jars (see page 39) | Large skillet | Sheet pan | Cut 4 large 12½-inch squares of foil or parchment paper

Make the **Chili Jam** first and leave it bubbling away while you prepare the rest of the meal | Clean out the food processor

Next, make the **Falafel** and set the first batch frying | Keep making them in batches until they are all cooked, transferring them to a sheet pan with a kitchen towel over the top in a 170°F oven to keep warm while you finish other jobs | Clean the skillet and food processor

Make your **Hummus**

Clean the work surface and dust it liberally with flour | Make and then cook the **Flatbreads**

Pick the flat-leaf parsley leaves, discard the stems, and chop the leaves

Place a **Flatbread** on a square of foil or parchment paper | Spread a generous layer of **Hummus** over the flatbread | Dollop over big spoonfuls of **Chili Jam** | Place 4 **Falafel** balls in a line across the middle of the flatbread and squish them a little bit with your fingers | Top the line of falafel balls with a few fresh spinach or salad greens, some onion pickle, and flat-leaf parsley | Roll up the wrap tightly and secure the top and bottom with more foil or parchment paper

Tear open and eat

FALAFEL

MAKES 16

Food processor | Large skillet | Line a large plate with paper towels

....

2 (14 oz) cans chickpeas
2 small red onions
3 garlic cloves
½ oz cilantro
½ oz fresh flat-leaf parsley
¾ cup all-purpose flour
2 tsp salt
1 tsp ground cumin
½ tsp black pepper
1½ tbsp harissa paste
½ lemon
olive oil, for frying

First get all your ingredients prepped | Drain the chickpeas, saving the water (aquafaba) for something else | Peel and roughly chop the red onions and garlic | Pick the leaves from the cilantro and parsley, discard the stems, and roughly chop

Now make the falafel mixture | Put all the ingredients except for the oil and lemon in the food processor | Squeeze in the lemon juice, catching any seeds in your other hand | Blitz to a thick paste

Using wet hands, divide the batter into 16 and roll into balls about 1¼ inches in diameter

Put the skillet over medium-high heat and add enough olive oil to cover the bottom of the pan | Once the oil is hot, carefully add the falafels and cook for 5–7 minutes, until golden all over and cooked through, turning regularly for even cooking (you may need to do this in batches) | Transfer to paper towels to drain before serving

3-INGREDIENT FLATBREADS

MAKES 4 THICK OR
8 THINNER FLATBREADS

Clean work surface dusted liberally with flour | Large skillet

....

3¾ cups plain flour, plus extra for dusting
1½ tsp salt
17 oz soy yogurt

To make the dough, put the flour and salt in a large mixing bowl and stir to combine | Make a well in the center and spoon in the yogurt | Combine with your hands to form a dough, making sure you incorporate all the flour | Tip onto the floured work surface and knead for a couple of minutes to bring the dough together (keep flouring the work surface and your hands to stop the dough sticking)

To make 4 thick flatbreads, divide the dough into 4 equal pieces and roll each one out to a circle 1/16–1/8 inch thick and the size of a dinner plate (or just a little smaller than your biggest skillet), adding more flour to the work surface as required | (To make 8 thinner ones, divide the dough into 8 and roll out to about a 1/16-inch thickness)

Put the pan over medium-high heat until hot | Carefully roll one of the flatbreads onto the rolling pin and transfer it to the pan | Cook for 2–3 minutes on each side | Repeat with the remaining flatbreads

CHILI JAM

MAKES ABOUT 4
HALF-PINT JARS

8 red bell peppers
12 fresh red chilies
1 Scotch bonnet chili, optional
2-inch piece fresh ginger
8 garlic cloves
1 (14.5 oz) can diced tomatoes
scant 4 cups superfine sugar
1 cup red wine vinegar

Food processor | Large saucepan | Sterilized jars (see page 39)

Start by getting your veg prepped | Cut the bell peppers in half and cut out the stems and seeds, then roughly chop | Rip the stems from the chilies, cut them in half lengthwise, and remove the seeds if you prefer a milder jam, then roughly chop | Peel the ginger by scraping off the skin with a spoon and roughly chop | Peel and roughly chop the garlic

Put the chopped ingredients into the food processor and pulse to finely chop

Tip the chopped vegetable into the saucepan and add all the rest of the ingredients | Put over high heat and bring to a boil | Use a spoon to remove any scum that rises to the surface | Simmer for 70–90 minutes, stirring occasionally to prevent sticking, until really thick

Transfer to sterilized jars, put the lids on, and leave to cool | Once opened, keep in the fridge and use within 1 month

HOLY TRINITY LOUISIANA GUMBO

We came back from one of our American trips with a real appetite for Southern comfort food and so gumbo had to make an appearance in this book. In this recipe we focus on the Holy Trinity of Cajun cooking: onions, bell peppers, and celery. It's also a good one to freeze—defrost overnight in the fridge and then reheat on the stove until piping hot.

SERVES 4

Large Dutch oven | Fine grater or Microplane

2 onions
2 celery stalks
2 green bell peppers
4 garlic cloves
10 oz okra
9 oz cremini mushrooms
4 tomatoes
2 sprigs fresh thyme
¼ cup olive oil
¼ tsp salt, plus a little extra
¼ cup all-purpose flour
1 tbsp tomato paste
1 tbsp apple cider vinegar
2 tsp smoked paprika
½ tsp cayenne pepper
1 tsp dried oregano
1 tsp Tabasco sauce
generous 3 cups vegetable stock
2 fresh bay leaves
1½ cups canned kidney beans
4 scallions
4 cups cooked basmati rice, or use
   2 (9 oz) bags microwavable
   basmati rice, for serving
black pepper

First get all your veg ready | Peel the onions | Trim the celery | Cut the bell peppers in half and cut out the stems and seeds | Roughly chop the onions, peppers, and celery into small pieces | Peel and finely grate the garlic | Trim the okra and cut into ⅓-inch-thick slices | Quarter the mushrooms | Finely chop the tomatoes | Roughly chop the thyme (if the stem is woody, remove the leaves by running your thumb and forefinger from the top to the base of the stem)

Put the Dutch oven over medium heat and pour in the oil | Once the dish is hot, add the onion, celery, peppers, and ¼ teaspoon salt | Sweat for about 10 minutes, until softened | Add the garlic, okra, and mushrooms and fry for 7–10 minutes longer, until the mushrooms are cooked through | Reduce the heat to medium-low, add the flour, and stir to combine | Cook for another 5–7 minutes, stirring constantly to avoid burning, until golden brown (don't stop cooking too early; this browning is what gives your gumbo its rich color)

Add the chopped tomatoes and tomato paste to the pan and stir for 2 minutes | Add the apple cider vinegar, thyme, smoked paprika, cayenne pepper, oregano, and Tabasco and stir for 2 minutes | Pour in the vegetable stock | Add the bay leaves and kidney beans, reduce the heat to a very gentle simmer, and cook for 30–35 minutes, until the broth is thick and hearty, stirring occasionally to make sure the bottom doesn't catch | Taste and season with salt and pepper

Heat the rice or cook it following the instructions on the package

Trim and thinly slice the scallions and sprinkle over the gumbo | Serve with the rice

TOFISH FINGER SANDWICH

A true shining star of a sandwich, this is our take on the classic British fish finger, combined with a quick tartar sauce and delightful mashy peas. Make more of the tartar sauce to keep in your fridge—it is great with our double-cooked fries on page 178 or a baked potato. The tofish fingers will keep really well in the freezer too.

MAKES 4

1 (15 oz) block extra-firm tofu
1 lemon
1 tsp salt
½ tsp black pepper
7 tbsp white wine vinegar
1 tbsp Dijon mustard
¾ cup all-purpose flour
generous ¾ cup unsweetened
    plant-based milk
1 cup breadcrumbs
olive oil, for frying
8 slices fresh crusty white bread
dairy-free butter, for spreading, optional
Speedy Tartar Sauce (see page 84)
ketchup, optional
Mashy Mashy Peas (see page 84)

Tofu press or 2 clean kitchen towels and a weight such as a heavy book | Fine grater or Microplane | Large saucepan | Line 2 plates with paper towels

....

Press the tofu using a tofu press or place it between two clean kitchen towels, lay it on a plate, and put a weight on top | Leave for at least 30 minutes to drain and firm up before you start cooking

Zest the lemon and squeeze the juice into the saucepan, catching the seeds with your other hand | Add the zest, ½ teaspoon of the salt, the black pepper, white wine vinegar, and mustard and mix | Drain any liquid from the tofu, cut it into 12 equal fingers, and add them to the pan, turning to cover | Leave to marinate for 30 minutes

Meanwhile, make the batter | Pour the flour, remaining ½ teaspoon salt, and the plant-based milk into a bowl and whisk to a batter | Put the breadcrumbs into another shallow bowl

Take the tofu fingers out of the marinade | Drop them into the batter and toss to coat completely | Transfer to the breadcrumbs and toss again, ensuring they are well covered | Place on a plate and set aside

Now get ready to cook the tofu | Quickly rinse the saucepan and pour in the olive oil until it's ¾ inch deep | Turn up the heat | Dip a wooden spoon into the oil and if bubbles form around the spoon, the oil is ready to cook | Carefully place the fingers in the oil and fry them in batches for 2–3 minutes, until golden and crispy all over | Transfer to the paper towels to soak up the excess oil

Build the sandwiches | Lay half the bread slices on plates and butter them if you prefer | Top with Speedy Tartar Sauce and ketchup, if using, the tofish fingers, and Mashy Mashy Peas | Cut in half and serve

MASHY MASHY PEAS

SERVES 4

Boiling water | Stick blender, optional

....

1½ cups frozen peas
1 tsp olive oil
1 tsp salt
1 tsp mint jelly or mint sauce

Pour the peas into a heatproof bowl, cover with boiling water, and leave for 5 minutes to thaw

In another bowl, combine the olive oil, salt, and mint jelly or sauce

Drain the peas, tip them into the mint mixture, and stir through | Crush the peas with a fork or give them a quick blitz with a stick blender

SPEEDY TARTAR SAUCE

SERVES 4

scant ½ egg-free mayonnaise
1 tbsp capers
1 small gherkin pickle
a pinch of salt
½ lemon

Put the dairy-free mayo into a small mixing bowl | Finely chop the capers and gherkin, add them to the bowl, and stir everything together

Taste and season with the salt and lemon juice, catching any seeds in your other hand as you squeeze the lemon half

GIANT BLT

These sandwiches are incredible. About half an hour after we posted this video on our channel a few BOSH! fans had already made it and sent us their pics! It's super-popular and we can see exactly why. Of course you can make this with regular-sized bread, but in true BOSH! style, we're making our sandwich big and bad. Why not take half to work with you?

SERVES 4

16 oz firm smoked tofu
3 tbsp cornstarch
2 tbsp smoked paprika
1 tsp garlic powder
1 tsp smoked salt (or normal salt)
2 tbsp maple syrup, plus 1 tbsp
    for glazing
2 tbsp soy sauce
1 large ciabatta
1 little gem lettuce
2 tomatoes
1 large avocado
6 tbsp egg-free mayonnaise
3 tbsp vegetable oil
2–3 tbsp red wine, for glazing
4 cornichons
salt and black pepper

Tofu press or 2 clean kitchen towels and a weight such as a heavy book | Deep-sided skillet | Line a large plate with paper towels | 4 toothpicks

Press the tofu using a tofu press or place it between two clean kitchen towels, lay it on a plate, and put a weight on top | Leave for at least 30 minutes to drain and firm up before you start cooking | Cut into ⅛-inch-thick slices

Preheat the oven to 350°F

Make a coating for the tofu | Put the cornstarch, smoked paprika, garlic powder, and salt into a mixing bowl and mix together with a fork | Roll the tofu slices in the dry mix and transfer to a plate | Drizzle the 2 tablespoons maple syrup and soy sauce over the prepared tofu slices and set to one side

Put the bread in the oven and leave for 5–7 minutes to warm through | Meanwhile, separate the lettuce leaves | Trim and thinly slice the tomatoes | Halve and carefully pit the avocado by tapping the pit firmly with the heel of a knife so that it lodges in the pit, then twist and remove | Scoop out the flesh with a spoon and slice thinly | Take the bread out of the oven and slice it in half through the middle

Spread both halves of the ciabatta with a generous layer of egg-free mayo | Layer the slices of lettuce, tomato, and avocado | Season with salt and pepper

Put the skillet over medium-high heat and pour in half the oil | When the pan is hot lay half the slices of tofu in the oil, then quickly but carefully add 1 tablespoon of red wine and ½ tablespoon of maple syrup | Toss the tofu in the glaze and fry until the liquid has evaporated and the tofu is well covered | Sprinkle with a small pinch of salt | Carefully turn the tofu slices over and sprinkle more salt on the other side | Fry until both sides are nice and browned, then transfer to the plate lined with paper towels to drain | Repeat to fry the remaining tofu, cleaning out the pan if necessary to prevent any residual maple syrup from burning

Lay the tofu bacon on top of the salad and put the lid on | Insert the toothpicks along the top of the sandwich and push a cornichon onto each one | Cut into four equal pieces and serve immediately

SWEET POTATO TIKKA MASALA

The tikka masala was once Britain's best-loved curry, only recently overtaken by jalfrezi (see page 74). This recipe will give you a true curry house taste, with its super-thick and creamy sauce. Make a double or triple batch of the sauce and freeze it, or keep it in the fridge for up to 2 days, for a super-speedy curry in a hurry. It goes well with the rotis on page 70.

SERVES 4–6

1½ lb sweet potatoes
3 tbsp vegetable oil
½ oz cilantro
1–2 fresh red chilies
2 red bell peppers
1 (13.5 oz) can full-fat coconut milk
hot chili powder, optional
½ lemon
a handful of sliced almonds
4 cups cooked basmati rice, or use
    2 (9 oz) bags microwavable
    basmati rice, for serving
rotis (store-bought or see page 70),
    optional
salt and black pepper

FOR THE CURRY SAUCE
2⅓-inch piece fresh ginger
5 garlic cloves
1 onion
1½ fresh red chilies
4 cherry tomatoes
¾ oz cilantro
1 tbsp vegetable oil
6 tbsp tomato paste
2 tbsp almond flour
2 tsp garam masala
1 tsp ground coriander
1 tsp ground cumin
1 tsp smoked paprika
1 tsp salt
a pinch of ground fenugreek
a pinch of ground turmeric
2 cups water

Preheat oven to 390°F | Line a sheet pan | Fine grater or Microplane | Medium saucepan | Blender

First roast the sweet potato | Peel the sweet potato and cut it into ¾-inch cubes | Put it on the sheet pan, pour over 2 tablespoons of the oil, toss to coat, and sprinkle with salt | Put into the hot oven for 20 minutes, turning occasionally, until soft and charring slightly at the edges | Remove and set aside

To make the curry sauce, peel the ginger by scraping off the skin with a spoon | Peel the garlic | Grate the ginger and garlic into a bowl and mix with a tablespoon of water | Peel and finely chop the onion | Finely chop the red chilies and tomatoes | Roughly chop the cilantro

Pour 1 tablespoon oil into the medium saucepan and place over medium-high heat | Add the onion and sauté for 5 minutes | Add the ginger garlic paste and fry for 30 seconds | Add all the remaining curry sauce ingredients except for the water and stir | Pour in half the water, stir, and simmer for 10 minutes, until browned and almost all the water has evaporated | Pour in the rest of the water, stir, then pour everything into the blender | Blend until smooth

Prepare the rest of the curry ingredients | Separate the leaves from the ½ ounce cilantro and chop roughly, then finely chop the stems | Rip the stems from the fresh red chilies and chop finely | Cut the bell peppers in half, cut out the stems and seeds, and chop into chunks

Splash 1 tablespoon oil into the same saucepan and place over high heat | Add the chopped cilantro stems, chili, and bell pepper and fry for 3 minutes, until slightly softened | Pour in the curry sauce and coconut milk | Add the roasted sweet potato and stir | Taste and add more salt and hot chili powder if you like it hot

Simmer for 10 minutes, until the sauce is nice and thick | Take off the heat and squeeze in the juice of half a lemon, catching any seeds in your other hand | Taste and season to perfection

Heat the rice or cook it following the instructions on the package

Plate up the tikka masala and garnish with the chopped cilantro leaves and sliced almonds | Serve immediately

MINI MUSHROOM PIES

These little cheeky pies are a great party snack or they are great served on a plate with some mushy peas (see page 84) and fries (see page 178). If you want to save some time, prepare the filling a day in advance, then store it overnight in an airtight container in the fridge.

SERVES 12

1 onion
1 leek
1 garlic clove
1 lb 10 oz cremini mushrooms
1 sprig fresh rosemary
2 sprigs fresh thyme
3 tbsp olive oil, plus extra for greasing
2 (11 oz) sheets ready-rolled plant-based
    puff pastry
salt and black pepper

FOR THE BÉCHAMEL
2 tbsp olive oil
¼ cup all-purpose flour
1½ cups unsweetened plant-based milk

Preheat oven to 390°F | Fine grater or Microplane | Large skillet | Saucepan | Stand blender or stick blender | Grease a 12-cup muffin tin with olive oil | 3-inch and 4-inch round pastry cutters (or something else to use as a template) | Pastry brush

. . . .

Start by preparing the veg | Peel and finely chop the onion | Trim and thinly slice the leek | Peel and grate the garlic | Quarter the mushrooms | Remove the leaves from the herbs by running your thumb and forefinger from the top to the base of the stems (the leaves should easily come away) and finely chop

Put the skillet over medium heat | Add 2 tablespoons oil | Add the onion and a pinch of salt and cook for 3–5 minutes, stirring | Add the leek and stir for 7–8 minutes | Add the garlic and stir for 1 minute | Add the mushrooms, rosemary, thyme, and 1 tablespoon oil and cook, stirring occasionally, for 10–12 minutes | Season to perfection | Increase the heat to high and cook for 10 minutes longer, until soft and all the liquid has evaporated | Remove from the heat and set aside

To make the béchamel, put the saucepan over medium heat and add the oil | Add the flour and stir vigorously for 2–3 minutes | Gradually add the milk, whisking constantly until smooth | Bring to a boil, then simmer for 2 minutes, until thickened | Blend half the mushroom mixture with the stick blender or in a stand blender until smooth | Add all the mushrooms to the pan and stir | Taste and season with salt and pepper

Unroll the pastry sheets and cut out twelve 4-inch rounds | Lightly press into the muffin cups so that there is some excess pastry peeping out from the tops | Divide the mushroom filling among the muffin cups | Cut out twelve 3-inch rounds, re-rolling the pastry as necessary | Top the pies with the rounds | Press the pastry rounds together tightly to seal and crimp the edges with a fork | Brush with olive oil and put in the oven | Bake for 25–30 minutes, until golden and crispy | Take out of the oven and let the pies cool in the tin for a moment before serving

PULLED JACKFRUIT SANDWICH

This sandwich is simply incredible. It harks back to Henry's youth, working at a music website and eating pulled pork sandwiches for lunch. The jackfruit makes for an amazingly tasty filling, which combines perfectly with the carrot crackling and sweet applesauce to produce perhaps the best sandwich we've ever created.

MAKES 4

2 tbsp olive oil
1 tsp salt
½ tsp black pepper
½ tsp sugar
2 tsp dried sage
1½ tsp onion powder
1½ tsp garlic powder
½ tsp dried parsley
2 (14 oz) cans young green jackfruit
   in water or brine
½ cup cooked plant-based bread stuffing
   (store-bought or make your own)
4 good-quality white bread rolls or
   English muffins
2 tbsp dairy-free butter
¼ cup applesauce

FOR THE CARROT CRACKLING
1 medium carrot
1 tbsp olive oil
½ tsp salt
½ tsp smoked paprika

Preheat oven to 390°F | Line 2 sheet pans

First roast the jackfruit | Add the olive oil, salt, pepper, sugar, sage, onion powder, garlic powder, and parsley to a large bowl and mix together with a fork | Drain the jackfruit and fold it into the mixture | Spread the seasoned jackfruit over one of the sheet pans, making sure it's well spaced out | Put the pan in the oven for 35–40 minutes, turning the jackfruit with tongs halfway through

If you're making your stuffing, follow the instructions on the package

Meanwhile, make the carrot crackling | Peel or thinly slice the carrot into long slices | Put in a bowl, drizzle in the olive oil, sprinkle with the salt and smoked paprika, and mix everything together to cover well | Spread on the second sheet pan, making sure the slices are well spaced out | When the jackfruit has been in the oven for 15 minutes, add the pan of carrot slices to the oven and continue to cook both for 20 more minutes | Keep an eye on the carrots as they may not need the full 20 minutes—they will start to crisp and brown slightly, but make sure they don't blacken | Remove any pieces that look cooked and return the softer ones to the oven | Take the pans out of the oven

Cut the bread rolls in half and spread them with dairy-free butter | Spread applesauce over the bottom halves and top each one with 2 tablespoons of stuffing | Shred the jackfruit by pulling it apart with two forks and divide among the rolls | Finish with a generous helping of carrot crackling | Close the sandwiches and serve

BOSH! BANGERS WITH MASH & QUICK ONION GRAVY

This is a slightly fiddly recipe but the payoff is so worth it. These homemade sausages are so delicious, they make for an incredibly comforting dinner. But if you don't have time, use store-bought sausages! We suggest doubling the recipe and freezing half the sausages, wrapped in foil and kept in an airtight container for up to a month. Defrost before cooking!

BOSH! BANGERS

MAKES 14 SMALL SAUSAGES (AROUND 2½ oz EACH)

2 carrots (about 10 oz)
1 parsnip (about 6 oz)
1 apple (about 5 oz)
5 garlic cloves
2 tbsp olive oil, plus more for greasing
1 onion
1 leek
a pinch of salt
5 tsp red wine
1 (14 oz) can cannellini beans
a large bunch of thyme
a large bunch of rosemary
1 cooked beet (around 2½ oz beet)
⅔ cup cooked brown basmati rice
3½ oz vital wheat gluten
1 tsp Dijon mustard
¼ tsp black pepper
a pinch of chili flakes

Preheat oven to 390°F | Line a sheet pan | Large sauté pan or saucepan | Food processor | Cut out 14 pieces of foil to make 10 x 4-inch rectangles | Steamer or large saucepan with a lid and a heatproof colander

....

Start by roasting the root veg and apple | Peel and chop the carrots, parsnip, and apple into ¾-inch pieces | Peel the garlic | Spread over the sheet pan and drizzle with 1 tablespoon of the oil | Put the pan in the oven and cook for 25−30 minutes, until soft and slightly caramelized

Meanwhile, peel and thiny slice the onion and leek | Pour the rest of the oil into the large pan and put the pan over medium heat | Add the onion and leek with a pinch of salt | Cook, stirring constantly, for 20−30 minutes, until the onions and leeks are dark and caramelized (caramelization occurs on the bottom of the pan) | Pour in the red wine and use a wooden spoon to scrape the bottom of the pan | Once the wine has reduced slightly, tip the mixture into the bowl of a food processor, scraping in any bits from the bottom of the pan

Add the roasted vegetables and apple to the food processor | Drain the cannellini beans | Remove the leaves from the herbs by running your thumb and forefinger from the top to the base of the stems (the leaves should easily come away) | Add the leaves to the bowl along with all the remaining ingredients and the drained beans | Pulse until the mixture comes together to form a dough (don't overwork the dough; it will come together quite quickly and look like bright pink bread dough)

Boil the water | Pour the boiling water into the steamer or a large pan with a colander placed over the top

Brush the foil rectangles lightly with olive oil | Divide the sausage mixture among the foil pieces, putting about 2½ oz in each one | Use your hands to roll them into sausage shapes and then wrap them in the foil, twisting tightly at each end to seal | Place the foil packages in the steamer or colander, put a lid on top, and cook for 45 minutes (you may need to do this in batches)

Continued next page

While the sausages are steaming, make the Incredible Mash, following the instructions below

Reheat the oven to 390°F | Re-line the sheet pan

When the sausages have steamed, take them off the heat, allow them to cool a little, and then carefully unwrap | Place on the lined pan and bake for 10 minutes, or until nice and browned

While the sausages are in the oven, make the Quick Onion Gravy (see opposite)

Spoon the smooth mash onto a serving plate or plates | Place the hot sausages on top | Pour onion gravy over the bangers and mash

INCREDIBLE MASH

SERVES 4

2¼ lb russet potatoes
3 garlic cloves
5 tbsp good-quality extra-virgin olive oil
2 tbsp unsweetened plant-based milk
2–4 tsp mustard, optional
salt and black pepper

Large saucepan | Potato ricer, food mill, or coarse sieve

Peel the potatoes and cut them into 1¼-inch chunks | Place them in the pan along with the unpeeled garlic cloves and cover with water | Add a pinch of salt | Place over high heat and bring to a boil | Cook for 15–17 minutes until tender | Drain well, remove the garlic cloves, and return the potatoes to the dry pan for a few seconds to steam and dry

Mash the potatoes, using a potato ricer or food mill if you have one, spooning in the mashed potatoes and milling or ricing them into a large bowl or back into the pan | Alternatively, spoon the mash into a large coarse sieve and use a spatula or large spoon to force them through | Gradually stir the olive oil and plant-based milk into the potatoes | Season generously with salt and pepper | Add mustard, if using, stirring in a teaspoon at a time until you are happy with the flavor

QUICK ONION GRAVY

SERVES 4

2 red onions
1 tbsp olive oil
3 garlic cloves
3 sprigs fresh rosemary
1 tsp maple syrup
⅔ cup red wine
¼ cup warm water
1 heaping tbsp flour
2 tbsp balsamic vinegar
1 vegetable bouillon cube
1½ cups boiling water

Large saucepan over medium heat | Fine grater or Microplane | Boiling water

....

Peel and thinly slice the red onions | Add the olive oil to the pan | Once the oil is hot, add the onions | Sauté for 7 minutes, stirring, until softened

Peel and grate the garlic and add to the pan | Cook for 1 minute

Meanwhile, remove the leaves from the rosemary by running your thumb and forefinger from the top to the base of the stems (the leaves should easily come away), finely chop, and add to the pan | Add the maple syrup and stir | Add the red wine | Increase the heat to medium, stir everything together, and let it bubble away for 8–10 minutes to evaporate the alcohol

Put the warm water into a bowl or mug and add the flour | Stir with a fork until all the lumps of flour are mixed in | Pour into the gravy | Add the vinegar, bouillon cube, and the boiling water | Bring to a boil, then reduce the heat and simmer, stirring often, for 5–7 minutes, until thickened (the gravy will thicken more as it cools)

ROAST SWEET POTATO TAGINE

Be whisked away to the Middle East with this hearty tagine. It's sweet, fragrant, and easy to make. You can replace the preserved lemon with the grated zest of a lemon, the juice of half a lemon, and an extra pinch of salt. It's also great with salad rather than the couscous for a lighter lunch.

SERVES 6

2¼ lb sweet potatoes
3 tbsp olive oil
2 medium red onions
1 fresh red chili
2 garlic cloves
2-inch piece fresh ginger
1 oz cilantro
3½ oz dried apricots
1⅓ cups canned chickpeas
2 tbsp harissa paste
2 tsp ras el hanout
2 tsp ground cumin
2 tsp ground coriander
½ tsp sugar
2 (14.5 oz) cans diced tomatoes
generous ¾ cup water
salt and black pepper

FOR THE LEMON & ALMOND COUSCOUS
1 preserved lemon
1½ tbsp extra-virgin olive oil
1 tsp ground cumin
10 oz couscous
1⅔ cups boiling water
½ cup sliced almonds
1 cup cilantro leaves

Preheat oven to 350°F | Line a sheet pan | Fine grater or Microplane | Large saucepan | Boiling water

First roast the sweet potato | Chop the sweet potatoes into 1¼-inch chunks | Spread over the sheet pan | Drizzle with 1 tablespoon of the olive oil and season with salt and pepper | Put in the oven and bake for 25 minutes

Meanwhile, peel and finely chop the red onions | Rip the stem from the chili, cut it in half lengthwise and remove the seeds, then finely chop | Peel and grate the garlic | Peel the ginger by scraping off the skin with a spoon and grate | Pluck the leaves from the cilantro, put them to one side, and thinly slice the stems | Roughly chop the dried apricots | Drain the chickpeas

To make the tagine, place the saucepan over medium heat and add the rest of the olive oil | Add the onions and fry for 4–5 minutes, stirring, until starting to soften | Add the chili, garlic, ginger, and chopped cilantro stems and stir for 2 minutes | Add the harissa paste, ras el hanout, cumin, ground coriander, and sugar and stir for 1 minute | Add the diced tomatoes and water | Lower the heat and simmer for 7–9 minutes | Stir in the chickpeas and apricots | Put the lid on and simmer for 8–10 minutes, stirring occasionally | Take the lid off the pan, taste and season | Add the cilantro leaves and roasted sweet potato and stir | Reduce the heat to low and put the lid back on the pan

To make the couscous, halve the preserved lemon and put it into a mixing bowl | Add the olive oil, cumin, couscous, and boiling water | Cover with a dinner plate and set aside for 8–10 minutes

Meanwhile, spread the sliced almonds over the sheet pan | Put in the oven and bake for 4 minutes, until lightly browned | Finely chop the cilantro leaves

Back to the couscous | Remove the preserved lemon and fluff the couscous with a fork | Reserve a quarter of the toasted almonds and a quarter of the chopped cilantro leaves and fold the rest into the couscous | Taste and season with salt and pepper

Divide the couscous among bowls and top with the tagine | Garnish with the reserved almonds and cilantro and serve

DOUGH 3 WAYS

This brilliantly versatile dough recipe can be used to make the pizzas, dough balls, and flatbreads on the following pages. It's such an easy way to cook up some comfort food! Keep a batch of dough in the freezer, wrapped in plastic wrap. Just remember to defrost it fully in the fridge before using.

MAKES ENOUGH FOR:
2 large pizzas (see page 102)
or 15 dough balls (see page 104)
or 4 flatbreads (see page 107)

3¾ cups bread flour, plus a little extra
half (7 g) envelope instant yeast
1½ tsp salt
1 cup + 7 tbsp water, at room
    temperature
vegetable oil or extra-virgin olive oil,
    for greasing

Clean work surface dusted liberally with flour | Plastic wrap

Measure the flour into a large bowl | Stir in the yeast and salt and mix well | Use your hands to make a well in the middle of the flour | Pour in the water and slowly mix together, kneading well with your fingers | Add more flour if necessary so that it's not too sticky

When the dough has come together, take it out of the bowl and put it on the floured work surface | Knead for 15 minutes, stretching and folding the dough, turning it 90 degrees, then repeating until it becomes really smooth and springy

Proof the dough | Wipe any flour or dough out of the bowl and rub the inside lightly with oil | Put the dough back in, cover the bowl with plastic wrap, and leave to rise for about 1 hour, until doubled in size | This is the first proof, and your dough is now ready be made into one of the following recipes

MARGHERITA PIZZA

Pizza has a special place in our hearts, and when we are feeling adventurous we'll top ours with a homemade cashew mozzarella. You can of course use a store-bought dairy-free cheese, but if you have the time, this one is excellent. The mozzarella will keep for a couple of days in the fridge. And, of course, this is pizza, so play around with your favorite toppings!

MAKES 2 LARGE PIZZAS

1 batch basic dough (see page 101)
20 fresh basil leaves, for garnish
semolina, for dusting

FOR THE MOZZARELLA
9 oz cashews
1¼ cups aquafaba (the drained water from 2–3 [14 oz] cans chickpeas)
3 tbsp coconut oil
5 tbsp tapioca flour
2 tbsp nutritional yeast
1 tsp salt
½ lemon

FOR THE TOMATO SAUCE
1 (14.5 oz) can diced tomatoes
1 garlic clove
3 tbsp fresh basil leaves
2 tsp dried oregano
½ tsp superfine sugar
a pinch of salt
a pinch of black pepper
1 tbsp olive oil
1 tbsp balsamic vinegar

Clean work surface dusted liberally with flour | Plastic wrap | Medium saucepan of hot water over high heat | Blender | Pizza stone or heavy baking sheet | Large baking sheet dusted with semolina | Rolling pin or clean, dry wine bottle

....

Tip the basic dough onto the floured work surface | Knead for 1 minute to knock it back, then divide it in two | Cover each half with plastic wrap and leave to proof for another 30 minutes

Meanwhile, make the mozzarella | Put the cashews in the pan of hot water and boil for 15 minutes, until they are soft and have rehydrated (alternatively, soak in cold water for at least 2 hours or ideally overnight)

Drain the cashews, then put all the ingredients for the mozzarella except for the lemon into the blender | Squeeze in the lemon juice, catching the seeds in your other hand | Blend to a smooth cream, then pour into the saucepan | Put the pan over medium heat and stir for 10–15 minutes, until the mixture is thick and gloopy | Transfer to a plate and form into a rough oblong shape with your hands | Leave to cool | Cut into about 8 equal pieces and shape into balls | Transfer to the fridge

Preheat the oven to 480°F | Put the pizza stone or heavy baking sheet on the middle rack of the oven to heat up | Clean out the blender | Dust the work surface with more flour

Add all the tomato sauce ingredients to the blender and blend to a smooth paste | Taste and season | Pour the sauce into the saucepan and simmer for 15 minutes, until thick

Roll one dough half out to make a pizza crust about 12 inches wide | Carefully roll it back onto the rolling pin and transfer to the baking sheet dusted with semolina | Spread over half the tomato sauce, leaving a 1-inch border around the edge

Take the mozzarella out of the fridge and slice the balls in half | Place half the slices over the pizza | Slide onto the hot pizza stone or baking sheet in the oven and bake for 10–12 minutes, until the crust has bubbled up and begun to darken | Prepare the second pizza

Slide the cooked pizza onto a wooden board or plate | Put the second pizza in to cook | Garnish the cooked pizzas with basil leaves and serve

CHEESEBURGER DOUGH BALLS

These little bites of heaven are amazing and taste just like cheeseburgers. They were a smash hit on our social media channels so we decided to bring them to life in this book! We recommend making double and freezing some for later. Simply pop them in an airtight container in the freezer instead of cooking them. Cook from frozen for 40–45 minutes.

MAKES 15

6 plant-based sausages
1 tsp garlic powder
1 tbsp Dijon mustard
½ tsp salt
½ tsp black pepper
olive oil, for drizzling and brushing
8 slices dairy-free cheese
1 batch basic dough (see page 101)
8 tsp red onion chutney
black sesame seeds, for sprinkling
ketchup, for dunking

Preheat oven to 350°F | Line a sheet pan | Microwavable plate, optional | Clean work surface dusted liberally with flour | Rolling pin or clean, dry wine bottle | Line a baking sheet with parchment paper | Pastry brush

....

First make the filling | Put the sausages on a microwavable plate | If they are frozen, cook on high for 90 seconds; if they're not frozen, cook for 20 seconds | Take the sausages out of the microwave and mash them with a fork to get them gooey and malleable | Alternatively, defrost the sausages in the fridge overnight, put them in the oven for 7 minutes, and mash with a fork

Transfer the mashed sausage to a bowl and add the garlic powder, mustard, salt and pepper, and mix | Divide into 15 equal portions and roll into balls | Place the balls on the sheet pan and flatten them into mini burger patties that are about 1½ inches wide and ¾ inch high | Drizzle with olive oil | Put the pan in the oven and bake for 10–12 minutes, until the patties are golden | Take the pan out of the oven and lay it on a heatproof surface

Meanwhile, cut the slices of dairy-free cheese into quarters

Tip the dough onto the floured work surface and knead for 1 minute to knock it back | Cut it into 15 equal portions and roll into balls | Roll each ball out to rounds, ¼ inch thick | Place a slice of cheese in the center of each round | Put ½ teaspoon red onion chutney on top of each slice of cheese and top with a mini burger | Top with another slice of cheese | Carefully fold up the edges of the dough rounds around the burgers, pinching the tops to neatly seal them

Flip over the dough balls and lay them sealed side down on the lined baking sheet | Brush liberally with olive oil and sprinkle with sesame seeds, gently pressing the seeds into the dough | Put the baking sheet in the oven and bake for 25–30 minutes, until golden brown

Remove from the oven, transfer to a plate, and serve with tomato ketchup to dunk in

KEBABISH TANDOORI SPECIAL

A kebab done well is a glorious thing, and though they often get a bad rep, when they're filled with veggies they can be incredibly healthy. These tandoori cauliflower chunks taste gorgeous—the combination of flavors inside one of these wraps is incredible. To save time on the day you can marinate your cauliflower florets overnight.

MAKES 4

1 head cauliflower (about 1½ lb)
½ oz fresh mint
½ cucumber
4 tomatoes
1 batch basic dough (see page 101)
hot sauce (store-bought or see page 161)

FOR THE TANDOORI MARINADE
3 garlic cloves
2-inch piece fresh ginger
7 oz coconut yogurt
2 tbsp vegetable oil
2 tsp garam masala
1 tsp smoked paprika
1 tsp ground turmeric
1 tsp ground cumin
1 tsp ground coriander
¾ tsp salt
½ tsp chili powder

FOR THE MINT RAITA
7 oz plant-based yogurt
½ tsp sugar
½ tsp salt
2 tsp jarred English mint sauce
⅛ tsp cayenne pepper
½ lemon

FOR THE QUICK RED ONION PICKLE
1 garlic clove
½ tsp sugar
½ tsp salt
7 tbsp clear vinegar (e.g., white wine or rice)
1 medium red onion

Preheat oven to 390°F | Line a large sheet pan and lay a wire cooling rack on top | Sieve or colander | Boiling water | Fine grater or Microplane | Clean work surface dusted liberally with flour | Large skillet | Rolling pin or clean, dry wine bottle | Cut out four 12-inch squares of foil or parchment paper

....

First make the pickle | Peel the garlic, cut it in half, and put it in a bowl | Add the sugar, salt, and vinegar and stir to dissolve | Peel and thinly slice the onion and put the slices in a colander over the sink | Pour boiling water over | Drain and add to the bowl | Stir to mix and set aside

Now make the marinade | Peel and grate the garlic | Peel the ginger then finely grate it | Put all the marinade ingredients into a large bowl and mix together | Taste and adjust the seasoning if necessary

Trim the cauliflower and break into 1¼-inch florets | Add to the marinade and mix well | Transfer the cauliflower to the cooling rack | Put the pan in the oven and bake for 25–30 minutes, until the cauliflower is darkening and getting crispy

Meanwhile, make the raita by putting the yogurt, sugar, salt, mint sauce, and cayenne into a bowl | Squeeze in the juice of the lemon, catching any seeds | Mix, taste, and adjust the seasoning if necessary

Pick the leaves from the mint and discard the stems | Coarsely chop the cucumber and tomatoes

Tip the risen basic dough onto the floured work surface and knead for 1 minute | Cut the dough in half and use one half for something else | Cut the rest into 4 equal pieces | Place the skillet over medium-high heat | Roll out one piece of dough until it is 10 inches wide and very thin, dusting with flour as you go | Once the pan is really hot, carefully lay the flatbread in the pan | Cook until light brown marks and bubbles appear on the bottom of the bread, 2–3 minutes | Flip and repeat | Transfer to a plate and leave to cool | Repeat to make all the breads

Lay out the foil or paper squares and place a flatbread on each | Spoon the raita, cucumber, tomatoes, and cauliflower down the middles | Add spoonfuls of onion pickle and sprinkle over the mint | Finish with a good helping of hot sauce and roll the kebabs tightly in the foil or paper | Rip open to enjoy

SHEPHERD'S PIE

This is perhaps one of Ian's favorite dishes: the British classic, shepherd's pie. Served with garden peas it is perfect for a cold winter evening. You can prepare the filling and mash the day before and keep them in separate airtight containers in the fridge, then assemble the pie when you're ready to cook it. It might take a few minutes longer if you're cooking it from cold.

SERVES 4–6

2 medium red onions
1 celery stalk
3 garlic cloves
4 sun-dried tomatoes,
    plus 2 tbsp oil from the jar
1 sprig fresh rosemary
3 sprigs fresh thyme
1 large carrot
1 lb mushrooms
2 tbsp tomato paste
1 tbsp yeast extract (e.g., Marmite)
1 tbsp balsamic vinegar
1 cup red wine
7 tbsp vegetable stock
2 cups precooked Puy lentils
salt and black pepper

FOR THE POTATO TOPPING
2 lb 10 oz russet potatoes
3 tbsp dairy-free butter
2/3 cup unsweetened plant-based milk
1 tbsp Dijon mustard

Preheat oven to 350°F | Fine grater or Microplane | 2 large saucepans | Food processor | Potato masher | 8 x 12-inch baking dish | Piping bag fitted with a wide star tip, optional

First make a start on the potato topping | Peel and chop the potatoes into large chunks | Put in a saucepan, cover with cold water, and add a generous pinch of salt | Put over high heat, bring to a boil, and cook for 12–15 minutes | Drain into a colander and leave to dry | Tip back into the pan

Now to the filling | Peel and finely dice the red onions and celery | Peel and grate the garlic | Finely chop the sun-dried tomatoes | Remove the leaves from the rosemary and thyme by running your thumb and forefinger from the top to the base of the stems (the leaves should easily come away), then finely chop | Peel and finely chop the carrot | Put the mushrooms in the food processor and blitz to mince

Put the second saucepan over medium heat | Pour in the sun-dried tomato oil | Add the onion and a small pinch of salt | Fry for 5 minutes, stirring | Add the garlic, sun-dried tomatoes, rosemary, and thyme and cook for 2 minutes | Add the carrot and celery and stir for 4–5 minutes | Add the mushrooms, turn up the heat slightly, and stir for 2–3 minutes, until the mushrooms start to sweat | Reduce the heat and cook for 5–7 minutes, stirring occasionally

Stir the tomato paste into the pan | Add the yeast extract and balsamic vinegar and stir for 1 minute | Add the red wine, stock, and lentils, turn up the heat, and simmer until most of the liquid has evaporated, about 10 minutes | Taste, season, and take off the heat

Mash the potatoes | Add the dairy-free butter, milk, and mustard to the potatoes and mash until really smooth | Taste and season

Spread the filling over the bottom of the baking dish | Spoon the potato into the piping bag, if using, and pipe tightly packed walnut-sized whips of potato all over; otherwise spoon over the potato and spread it out with the back of a spoon, then drag a fork over it to make rows that will catch and brown in the oven

Put the pie in the oven and bake for 25–30 minutes, until starting to crisp and turn golden brown | Remove and serve

FEASTS

Henry's favorite
Easy Peasy Roast Dinner

Ian's favorite
Classic Lasagna

CLASSIC LASAGNA

Lasagna will always be one of our favorites, and this simple mushroom ragu with a rich, creamy béchamel is a real classic. We don't think you should mess with perfection, but you could add a few chili flakes if you like. The ragu and béchamel can be made the day before and kept in the fridge, so on the day you just have to build and bake the final dish.

SERVES 6—8

2 onions
3½ oz sun-dried tomatoes, plus 2 tbsp oil from the jar
3 carrots
3 celery stalks
1 sprig fresh rosemary, plus more for garnish
2 sprigs fresh thyme
4 garlic cloves
1½ lb cremini mushrooms
1¼ cups red wine
1 tbsp tomato paste
1 tbsp red miso paste
1 tsp balsamic vinegar
½ tsp dried oregano
2 tsp soy sauce
2 (14.5 oz) cans diced plum tomatoes
3⅓ cups water
1 lb oven-ready lasagna sheets
salt and black pepper
field greens, for serving

FOR THE BÉCHAMEL
½ cup olive oil
1 cup flour
5¼ cups unsweetened plant-based milk
1½ tbsp nutritional yeast

Food processor | 2 large saucepans, one over medium heat | Fine grater or Microplane | 10 x 12-inch baking lasagna dish | Foil

Peel and quarter the onions and blitz them in the food processor until finely chopped | Add the sun-dried tomato oil to the large pan on the heat and sauté the onions, stirring, for 5—6 minutes

Meanwhile, peel the carrots and pulse them in the food processor with the celery until minced | Remove the leaves from the rosemary and thyme and finely chop | Peel and grate the garlic and add it to the pan | Stir for 1 minute | Add the carrot, celery, rosemary, and thyme, reduce the heat slightly, and sauté, stirring occasionally, for 12—15 minutes

Meanwhile, thinly slice the sun-dried tomatoes | Pulse the mushrooms in the food processor until finely minced | Add to the pan along with the sun-dried tomatoes | Stir, increase the heat slightly, and sauté, stirring, for 8—10 minutes

Pour in the wine, increase the heat, and stir constantly for 5—6 minutes, until nearly all the liquid has evaporated | Add the tomato paste, miso paste, balsamic vinegar, oregano, and soy sauce and stir for 1 minute | Add the diced tomatoes and water | Lower the heat to medium and simmer for 30 minutes | Taste and season

While it is simmering, make the béchamel | Put the second pan over medium heat and add the olive oil | Add the flour and stir for 3—5 minutes | Gradually add the milk, stirring constantly | Add the nutritional yeast and stir until smooth | Bring to a boil, then lower the heat and simmer until the béchamel thickens to the consistency of custard | Taste and season | Preheat the oven to 350°F

Now, layer up your lasagna | Spread a quarter of the ragu into the baking dish | Spoon over a quarter of the béchamel | Cover with lasagna sheets, breaking them if necessary to make a complete layer with no gaps | Repeat three times, reserving some béchamel to cover the top completely | Garnish with a few rosemary leaves | Cover with foil and put on the lowest shelf of the oven | Bake for 50 minutes | Remove the foil and bake for 15 minutes longer | Leave to stand for 10 minutes before serving with the salad greens | The leftovers will taste amazing the next day—simply bring back to piping hot in the oven or microwave

SEASIDE ROLL WITH SALSA VERDE & NEW POTATOES

This seaside roll is our plant-based take on a salmon en croûte and is a beautiful, exciting centerpiece. The salsa verde gives a fresh zing to the new potatoes and is the perfect side sauce for the crispy seaside roll. Pressing your tofu is really important here as we don't want the pastry to become soggy.

SERVES 8

1 (14 oz) block firm tofu
3 garlic cloves
1 lemon
1½-inch piece fresh ginger
3 roasted red peppers from a jar
1 tbsp olive oil, plus more for glazing
1 tsp salt, plus extra to season
½ large cucumber
2 scallions
½ oz fresh dill
1 tbsp Dijon mustard
½ tbsp white wine vinegar
1 tsp light agave nectar
2 oz watercress, plus extra to serve
1 (12 oz) sheet ready-rolled plant-based puff pastry
unsweetened plant-based milk, for brushing
black pepper

FOR THE SALSA VERDE
1 oz fresh parsley
1 oz fresh mint
2 small garlic cloves
3 tbsp capers
1 large gherkin pickle
1 tbsp Dijon mustard
3 tbsp red wine vinegar
⅔–¾ extra-virgin olive oil
salt and black pepper

FOR THE NEW POTATOES
2 lb 10 oz new potatoes
a large pinch of salt
¾ cup fresh parsley leaves
⅔ cup fresh dill leaves
3 tbsp olive oil
salt and black pepper

Tofu press or 2 clean kitchen towels and a weight such as a heavy book | Fine grater or Microplane | Food processor | Baking sheet | Large saucepan

Press the tofu using a tofu press or place it between two clean kitchen towels, lay it on a plate, and put a weight on top | Leave for at least an hour to drain and firm up | Preheat oven to 350°F

Make the tofu filling | Peel the garlic | Zest and juice the lemon | Peel and grate the ginger | Put the roasted red peppers, tofu, oil, garlic, lemon juice and zest, ginger, and 1 teaspoon salt into the food processor and pulse until combined | Season with salt and pepper

Prepare the cucumber filling | Cut the cucumber in half lengthwise, scrape out the seeds, and cut into ⅓-inch-thick slices | Thinly slice the scallions | Finely chop the dill | Place the cucumber, scallions, mustard, white wine vinegar, agave nectar, dill, and watercress in a bowl, season with salt and pepper, and set aside

Unroll the pastry and lay it on its paper on the baking sheet | Spread half the tofu mixture neatly, lengthwise, down one side of the pastry, leaving a ¾-inch border | Cover the tofu with the cucumber mixture and then another layer of tofu | Neaten the filling so that it's firm and smooth | Brush the edges of the pastry with plant-based milk | Gently pull the exposed pastry up and over the filling | Press along the edge to seal, then crimp with a fork | Using a sharp knife make a crosshatch pattern across the top, as well as a few slits | Brush with olive oil | Put the baking sheet in the oven for 35–40 minutes, until golden and crispy | Remove from the oven

Meanwhile, make the salsa verde | Clean out the food processor | Separate the herb leaves and discard the stems | Put the leaves in the food processor | Peel the garlic and add to the herbs with the capers and gherkin | Pulse to finely chop | Remove the blade | Add the mustard and vinegar and mix well | Gradually stir in the oil until you reach your desired consistency | Taste and season

Put the new potatoes in the large saucepan, cover with cold water, and sprinkle in the salt | Put over high heat and boil for 10–12 minutes, until tender | Roughly chop the parsley and dill leaves | Drain the potatoes and tip them back into the pan | Drizzle with the olive oil | Sprinkle in the herbs | Season and toss to coat

Slice the Seaside Roll | Serve with potatoes, salsa verde, and watercress

PAN-FRIED SEITAN STEAK WITH SECRET SAUCE

This steak is succulent and satisfying and the secret sauce is out of this world! You'll impress all of your carnivore friends. Serve with our Double-Cooked Rosemary Fries (see page 178) and a side salad for the perfect fancy dinner. For a drier, firmer texture press the steak as you would tofu—wrapping it in kitchen paper and placing a weight on top for 20 minutes.

SERVES 4

6 oz vital wheat gluten
¾ cup precooked Puy lentils
2 tbsp nutritional yeast
2 tbsp tomato paste
1 tbsp garlic powder
1 tbsp chili powder
1 tbsp soy sauce
½ tsp smoked salt
½ tsp black pepper
6 tbsp water
a splash of oil
5 oz fries per person, for serving

FOR THE MARINADE
2 tbsp olive oil
1 tbsp soy sauce
1 tbsp maple syrup

Food processor | Clean work surface | Large saucepan of salted water over high heat | Large freezer bag | Sauté pan

First make the steak | Add all the ingredients, apart from the water and oil, to the food processor and pulse to combine | Add the water and blitz, scraping down the sides as needed | Tip the mixture onto a clean work surface, knead for a minute or two, then bring it together into a tight ball

Roll the mixture into a rough oblong shape and cut into 4 even slices | Flatten each slice with your hand so they're roughly ⅓ inch thick and steak-shaped (you can also use a rolling pin here) | For a drier texture press the steak as you would tofu—wrapping it in paper towels, and placing a weight on top of it for 20 minutes, which will give a firmer texture

Lower the steaks into the pan of boiling salted water and simmer for 25 minutes | Take the steaks out of the pan, drain, and leave to cool for 5 minutes

Put the ingredients for the marinade into a large freezer bag | Put the steaks in the bag and roll them around in the marinade so they are well coated | Leave to marinate for 20 minutes | While the steaks are marinating, make the Café de Paris Secret Sauce (see opposite)

When you're ready to cook the steaks place a sauté pan over medium-high heat | Add a splash of oil and let it get hot | Add the steaks and pour over any remaining marinade | Cook for 2–3 minutes on each side, basting the steaks with the oil in the pan as they cook | Remove when both sides are well browned, but the steak is still tender | Leave to rest for a couple of minutes before serving with fries and Secret Sauce served on the side (as in the photo)

Pictured on pages 118—119

CAFÉ DE PARIS SECRET SAUCE

MAKES ABOUT 1¼ CUPS

Saucepan | Blender

2 large shallots
3 garlic cloves
½ oz fresh tarragon
1 tsp capers
1½ tbsp olive oil
2 cups + 2 tbsp vegetable stock
¼ cup white wine
3 tbsp red wine vinegar
2 tbsp Dijon mustard
1 tsp soy sauce
1 tsp black pepper
1 tsp salt

Prep the ingredients | Peel and thinly slice the shallots | Peel and finely chop the garlic | Pick the tarragon leaves, discard the stems, then finely chop | Finely chop the capers

Put the saucepan over medium heat | Add 1 tablespoon of the olive oil | Add the garlic and shallots and cook for 4–5 minutes until soft, stirring occasionally | Add the vegetable stock and simmer for 3–4 minutes | Add all the remaining ingredients and bring to a boil, then simmer for 10 minutes until the sauce has reduced a little and become thicker | Take the pan off the heat and set aside to cool to room temperature

Pour the sauce into the blender and blend until smooth | Pour back into the pan and bring to a simmer | Stir in the remaining ½ tablespoon olive oil before serving

HENRY'S BIRYANI WITH CILANTRO CHUTNEY

This dish is a revelation. Jackfruit is a traditional Indian ingredient and it does an incredible job of soaking up the aromatic spices. You can use whatever vegetables you like though—1¾ lb sweet potatoes, pumpkin, or any mix of veg would be perfect. Simply boil or roast until softened but still a little firm, then use them in place of the jackfruit.

SERVES 6

1 cup basmati rice

2 cups boiling water

10 green cardamom pods

7 garlic cloves

3 fresh bay leaves

3 cinnamon sticks

2 (14 oz) cans young green jackfruit in water or brine

2 onions

1¼-inch piece fresh ginger

¼ tsp black peppercorns

½ cup vegetable oil

1 tsp red chili powder

2 tsp ground coriander

1 tsp ground cumin

1 tsp ground turmeric

½ cup dairy-free yogurt

Cilantro Chutney ingredients (see page 122)

Mint Raita (see page 107), optional

salt

Preheat oven to 350°F | Boiling water | Small saucepan with a tight-fitting lid over medium heat | Sauté pan | Line a plate with paper towels | Small roasting pan | Foil

First cook the rice | Rinse the rice under cold running water until the water runs clear | Drain and tip into the saucepan | Pour over 1⅔ cups of the boiling water | Add a pinch of salt, 6 of the cardamom pods, 4 garlic cloves, 2 bay leaves, and 2 cinnamon sticks | Turn up the heat and bring to a boil, stir once, then reduce the heat to the lowest setting | Put the lid on and cook for 6 minutes | Don't touch the rice until the time is up | Take the pan off the heat, drain the rice in a sieve, then tip it back into the pan and put the lid on

Drain the jackfruit | Peel and thinly slice the onions and remaining 3 garlic cloves | Peel the ginger by scraping off the skin with a spoon and chop finely | Crush the remaining cardamom pods and the peppercorns

Place the sauté pan over high heat and add ¼ cup of the oil | Add the onions to the hot pan, sprinkle with a pinch of salt, and fry, stirring constantly, for 10 minutes, until the onions are dark and crispy, but not burnt | Transfer to the paper towels

Add 2 tablespoons more oil to the pan | Add the remaining 1 bay leaf, the sliced garlic cloves, cinnamon stick, crushed cardamom, and peppercorns and fry for 2 minutes | Add the jackfruit and roughly pull the strands apart with a fork | Fry for 2 minutes, stirring continuously | Add the ginger, chili powder, ground coriander, cumin, and turmeric and fry for 5 minutes more | Taste and season | Add the yogurt and generous ⅓ cup boiling water to the pan | Lower the heat to medium and stir for 2–3 minutes | Taste and season, then remove from the heat

Continued next page

Spoon a layer of rice over the bottom of the roasting pan | Add a layer of jackfruit | Sprinkle on a spoonful of the onions | Repeat this layering to use up all the ingredients, finishing with a layer of rice, with some jackfruit and onion peeping through | Drizzle the remaining oil over the biryani, cover with foil, and put the pan in the oven | Bake for 20–25 minutes

While the biryani is baking, make your Cilantro Chutney, following the instructions below

Take the pan out of the oven and remove the foil | Spoon the biryani into bowls or plates, drizzle on the Cilantro Chutney, and serve immediately with some raita on the side

CILANTRO CHUTNEY

MAKES ABOUT 4 oz

4 scallions
¾-inch piece fresh ginger
1 small fresh red chili
1 oz cilantro
6 tbsp fresh mint leaves
¾ tsp salt
½ tsp sugar
½ tsp garam masala
¼ tsp cayenne pepper
2 tbsp vegetable oil
1 tbsp water
1 lemon

Blender

First get your ingredients ready | Trim and roughly chop the scallions | Peel the ginger by scraping off the skin with a spoon and chop roughly | Rip the stem from the chili

Put all the ingredients except for the lemon in the blender | Zest the lemon into the blender and then cut it in half and squeeze in the juice, catching any seeds with your other hand | Blend everything together and then check the consistency, adding more water if it's too thick | Transfer to a bowl and serve | This chutney is also great with pappadums

EASY PEASY ROAST DINNER

This is such a good roast dinner, with the awesome jackfruit taking center stage. It takes a little while, but most of the time it's your oven that's doing all the hard work! The process for making the jackfruit is similar to the jackfruit sandwich on page 92, so you could double up on this one and have leftovers for delicious jack and carrot crackling sandwiches the next day!

SERVES 4

Herb Oil ingredients (see page 127)
Roasted Root Vegetables ingredients
   (see page 126)
Pulled Jackfruit ingredients
   (see page 126)
6 oz store-bought plant-based bread
   stuffing
Red Wine Gravy ingredients (see page
   127)
small jar store-bought applesauce

Preheat oven to 390°F | Line 1 sheet pan | 1 large saucepan with a lid | Colander | Boiling water | Blender | Roasting pan

Make your **Herb Oil** following the instructions on page 127

Then get your **Roasted Root Vegetables** in the oven on the top shelf, following the instructions on page 126

Next, make your **Pulled Jackfruit** and get that in the oven on the middle shelf, following the instructions on page 126

Next, prepare your stuffing following the instructions on the package | Put in the oven on the bottom shelf

While they're all roasting, make your **Red Wine Gravy**, following the instructions on page 127

Serve piping hot with the applesauce on the side

Pictured on pages 124—125

PULLED JACKFRUIT

SERVES 4

3 (14 oz) cans young green jackfruit
    in water or brine
5 tbsp Herb Oil (see opposite) or olive oil
½ tsp salt
1 tsp black pepper
1 tsp sugar
4 tsp dried sage
3 tsp onion powder
3 tsp garlic powder
½ tsp smoked paprika
1 tsp dried parsley

Preheat oven to 390°F | Line a sheet pan | Clean kitchen towel or paper towels

. . . .

Drain the jackfruit, rinse under a cold tap, and pat dry with a clean kitchen towel or paper towels

Put all the ingredients except for the jackfruit into a large mixing bowl and mix with a fork | Add the jackfruit and toss to coat it in the seasoning

Spread out the seasoned jackfruit on the sheet pan, making sure the pieces are well spaced out | Put the pan in the oven to cook for 35–40 minutes, or until very lightly charred and crispy, turning the jackfruit halfway through | Remove from the oven, transfer to a bowl, and serve immediately

ROASTED ROOT VEGETABLES

SERVES 4

2 lb russet potatoes
5–6 carrots (about 1 lb)
3–4 parsnips (about 1 lb)
4 large shallots
1 garlic bulb
½ cup Herb Oil (see opposite) or olive oil
4 sprigs fresh rosemary
8 sprigs fresh thyme
salt and black pepper

Preheat oven to 390°F | Large roasting pan | Large saucepan

. . . .

Peel the vegetables | Cut the potatoes into quarters | Cut the carrots and parsnips into 1¼-inch chunks | Peel and quarter the shallots | Break the garlic bulb into individual cloves, but don't peel them

Pour the oil into the roasting pan, put the pan in the oven, and leave it to heat up for 10 minutes

Meanwhile, add the potatoes and carrots to the saucepan, cover with cold water, and throw in a generous pinch of salt | Put the pan over high heat, bring to a boil, and cook for 4 minutes | Add the parsnips and cook for 4 minutes longer | Tip the veggies into a colander, tossing them around to rough up the edges | Set aside

Take the pan out of the oven and set it down on a heatproof surface | Carefully spoon the veggies into the pan and roll them around in the hot oil to make sure they're well coated | Sprinkle in the shallots, garlic cloves, rosemary, and thyme and season with salt and pepper | Put the pan in the oven to roast for about 1 hour, stirring every 20 minutes to ensure an even, crispy cook | Remove from the oven and serve

HERB OIL

MAKES ABOUT 2 CUPS

4 sprigs fresh rosemary
8 sprigs fresh thyme
1 tsp salt
½ tsp black pepper
2 cups peanut or canola oil

Blender | Sterilized bottle (see page 39)

Remove the leaves from the herbs by running your thumb and forefinger from the top to the base of the stems (the leaves should easily come away), then finely chop | Put all the ingredients into the blender | Blend until smooth and then leave to rest for 10 minutes | Pour through a sieve into a measuring cup | Use immediately or pour into the bottle and refrigerate | Use within a week

RED WINE GRAVY

MAKES ABOUT 2½ CUPS

2 red onions
3 garlic cloves
2 carrots
2 celery stalk
2 tbsp Herb Oil (see above) or olive oil
1 sprig fresh rosemary
2 sprigs fresh thyme
1 cup red wine
1 tbsp tomato paste
1 tsp yeast extract (e.g., Marmite)
1 tsp mustard
4¼ cups vegetable stock
2 tbsp water
3 tbsp all-purpose flour
salt and black pepper

Fine grater or Microplane | Medium saucepan | Large heatproof bowl with a sieve on top

First prep the veg | Peel and roughly chop the red onions | Peel and finely grate the garlic | Peel and coarsely grate the carrots | Thinly slice the celery

Put the saucepan over medium-low heat and add the oil | Add the onions to the hot pan and fry for 5 minutes, stirring, until starting to soften | Add the garlic and stir for 1 minute | Add the carrot and celery and fry for 15–17 minutes, stirring every minute to ensure nothing sticks to the pan | Add the herbs and wine | Turn up the heat and cook until most of the liquid has evaporated | Add the tomato paste, yeast extract, and mustard and stir | Pour in the vegetable stock, bring to a boil, reduce the heat, and leave to simmer for 10–12 minutes | Strain the liquid through the sieve into the bowl | Wipe the pan clean | Pour the strained liquid back into the pan and put it back on the heat

Add the water to a mug | Add the flour and whisk with a fork or whisk until there are no lumps | Pour into the pan and whisk to combine | Simmer, whisking all the time, for 5 minutes, until thickened | Taste, season, and serve

ULTIMATE NUT ROAST

This is no ordinary nut roast. This is richly flavored, amazingly moist, and will make a wonderful centerpiece at any roast dinner. Use a food processor for chopping the veg to speed up the prep time, or you can even make the whole nut roast the day before — just give it 5–10 more minutes if you're cooking it straight from the fridge.

SERVES 8

3½ oz walnuts
3½ oz pecans
3½ oz hazelnuts
3½ oz cooked chestnuts
2 large parsnips (about 14 oz)
2 red onions
3 garlic cloves
1 fresh red chili
1 carrot (about 5 oz)
3½ oz cremini mushrooms
8 sprigs fresh thyme
2 sprigs fresh rosemary
1 sprig fresh sage
2 tbsp olive oil
1 cup whole wheat breadcrumbs
generous ¾ cup vegetable stock
¼ tsp ground nutmeg
¼ tsp ground allspice
¼ tsp smoked paprika
1 clementine
3 tbsp dried cranberries
sea salt and black pepper
fresh cranberries, to decorate

Preheat oven to 350°F | Grease and line a 9 × 5-inch loaf pan with parchment paper | Sheet pan | Medium saucepan of boiling salted water over high heat | Potato masher | Fine grater or Microplane | Deep-sided skillet | Food processor | Foil

Spread the walnuts, pecans, and hazelnuts over a sheet pan | Put the pan in the oven for 8 minutes | Set aside to cool | Crumble the chestnuts

Peel and chop the parsnips into ¾-inch cubes | Add them to the pan of salted water and cook for 15–18 minutes, until tender | Take off the heat, drain, and tip back into the pan | Mash

Prepare the rest of the veg and herbs | Peel and finely chop the red onions | Peel and grate the garlic | Rip the stem from the chili and slice thinly | Peel and finely grate the carrot | Finely chop the mushrooms | Remove the leaves from the herbs by running your thumb and forefinger from the top to the base of the stems (the leaves should easily come away) | Reserve a few sprigs of thyme for garnish and finely chop the rest

Place the skillet over medium heat and add the oil | Add the onions and stir for 15 minutes, until really brown and caramelized, stirring regularly to prevent burning | Add the garlic and chili and cook for 1 minute | Add the carrot and mushrooms and cook until the mushrooms are sweating and the carrot is softening, about 10 minutes | Add the breadcrumbs, vegetable stock, chopped herbs, and spices and fold them into the rest of the ingredients | Take the pan off the heat

Pour half the roasted nuts into the food processor and blitz to a meal | Finely chop the rest of the nuts | Add all the nuts to the pan | Zest the clementine into the pan (you can eat the fruit) | Tip in the mashed parsnips and dried cranberries and fold everything together to form a thick, textured dough | Taste and season

Tip the mixture into the prepared loaf pan and smooth the top with a spatula | Cover with foil | Put the pan in the oven and bake for 80 minutes, removing the foil after 1 hour

Take the pan out of the oven and leave to cool for 30 minutes | Carefully remove the nut roast from the pan, and decorate with the reserved thyme sprigs and some fresh cranberries | Sprinkle with sea salt and serve with all the trimmings

BOSH XMAS

Our Christmas table looks just like the one on pages 132–133, and in the middle is our amazing Crisscross that will be sure to impress your guests. There's quite a lot to make and prep here, so follow the timings below for a perfect festive feast. The recipes are also great on their own as sides for other meals, so don't just save them for the big day!

SERVES 8

Christmas Crisscross ingredients
   (see page 134)
2 batches Brussels Sprouts with
   Maple Mushrooms (see page 137)
Ultimate Roast Stuffing Balls
   (see page 142)
2 batches Clementine Roasted Root
   Vegetables (see page 138)
Perfect Gravy (see page 143)
2 batches Crisp, Fluffy, Perfect Roast
   Potatoes (see page 141)
2 batches Bangers in Blankets
   (see page 137)
cranberry sauce, for serving, optional
mint sauce, for serving, optional

Christmas Eve: Preheat oven to 350°F | line 3 sheets pans | Food processor | Deep skillet | 4 large airtight containers or several smaller ones | 3 roasting pans | 2 large saucepans | Foil | Potato masher or stick blender

....

First get the mushrooms for your **Christmas Crisscross** into the oven | Prep the **Maple Mushrooms** and put them in the oven | Prep the rest of the filling for the **Crisscross** | Put the walnuts for the **stuffing** in the oven

Take the walnuts and mushrooms for the **Maple Mushrooms** out of the oven and let them cool | Take out the mushrooms for the **Crisscross** and leave to cool | Transfer to separate containers, label them, and put them in the fridge | Clean out the food processor

Turn the oven up to 375°F | Prep the beets for the **roast vegetables** and put them in the oven on the top shelf | Prep the vegetables for the **Perfect Gravy** and put them on the middle shelf | Prep the carrots for the **roast veg** and put them on the bottom shelf

Meanwhile, continue making your stuffing mixture | Boil your **Brussels**, drain, cool, label, and refrigerate | Keep an eye on the veg in the oven and take them out when they're cooked | Nestle the beets into the carrots and set them aside to cool, cover with foil, and leave overnight (or label and refrigerate) | Lower the oven to 350°F

Roll your **stuffing balls** and bake them | Let them cool, cover in foil, and leave in the fridge overnight

Meanwhile, finish making your **gravy** | Turn off the heat, put a lid on the pan, and leave overnight

Prep and boil your **potatoes**, steam dry, and transfer to a container

Christmas Day: Preheat oven to 350°F | Foil | 1 baking sheet | 3 more sheet pans | Skillet | Pastry brush, optional | At least 12 toothpicks | Line 2 plates with paper towels

In the morning, take all the food out of the fridge to come up to room temperature

Whack the oven up to 425°F and get your **potatoes** in on the middle shelf

Construct your **Crisscross** and put it in the fridge

Prep your **Bangers in Blankets** so that they're ready to go in the oven

Take the **potatoes** out, loosely cover with foil, and set aside | Lower the heat to 350°F

Put the **Crisscross** on the middle shelf of the oven for 25 minutes | Put the baked almonds for the **Brussels** in for the last 10 minutes

Take out the mushrooms | Take out the almonds, tip them onto a plate, and tip the walnuts for the **roasted vegetables** onto the pan | Glaze the **Crisscross**, then put it back in | Put the **Bangers in Blankets** on the bottom shelf | Put the walnuts on the top shelf

After 10 minutes, remove the walnuts and put the **roasted veg** in, uncovered | Chop the walnuts | Put the gravy on to heat up

Bring water to a boil and pour the water over the **Brussels** to warm them up | Drain and finish cooking the dish

Take the **Crisscross** and **roasted veg** out of the oven | Put the **potatoes** back in the oven to warm up | Put the stuffing in the oven to heat through | Add the walnuts and beet to the **roasted veg**

Pile your **Brussels** into a serving bowl | Stack your **Bangers in Blankets** and **Stuffing Balls** high on plates | Serve your **roasted vegetables** and **Crisp, Fluffy, Perfect Roast Potatoes** on their pans | Pour your **Perfect Gravy** into a jug | Get everyone seated and bring in your **Christmas Crisscross** | Merry Christmas!

Pictured on pages 132–133

CHRISTMAS CRISSCROSS

SERVES 8

1 lb cremini mushrooms

olive oil, for drizzling

8 sprigs fresh thyme

4 sprigs fresh rosemary

2 sprigs fresh sage

8 garlic cloves

4 large shallots

1 carrot

1 celery stalk

4 sun-dried tomatoes, plus 3 tbsp oil from the jar

7 oz cooked chestnuts

7 oz pecans

generous ¾ cup red wine

2½ tbsp cranberry sauce

1 bay leaf

½ tsp ground nutmeg

½ tsp ground cinnamon

1 cup dried breadcrumbs

2 (11 oz) sheets ready-rolled plant-based puff pastry

1 tbsp maple syrup

2 tbsp unsweetened plant-based milk, plus extra for brushing

salt and black pepper

Preheat oven to 350°F | Foil | Roasting pan | Fine grater or Microplane | Food processor | Deep-sided skillet | Baking sheet | Pastry brush, optional

Start by cooking the mushrooms | Lay a sheet of foil over the roasting pan | Sort through the mushrooms and find 10 of the best-looking ones, making sure you're left with about 10 oz mushrooms | Place the selected mushrooms in the middle of the foil | Drizzle with a little olive oil and sprinkle with a little salt and pepper | Lay half the thyme, rosemary, and sage sprigs on top along with 3 of the garlic cloves | Wrap the mushrooms tightly in the foil and put the pan in the oven | Bake for 30 minutes

Meanwhile, prep the rest of the veg and herbs | Peel and thinly slice the shallots | Peel and finely grate the carrot | Finely dice the celery | Thinly slice the sun-dried tomatoes | Peel and finely grate the rest of the garlic cloves | Remove the leaves from the remaining thyme and rosemary sprigs by running your thumb and forefinger from the top to the base of the stems (the leaves should easily come away), then finely chop | Pick the leaves from the sage sprig and finely chop

Put the remaining mushrooms in the food processor and blitz to mince | Scrape into a bowl and clean out the food processor | Add half the chestnuts and all of the pecans to the clean food processor and blitz to a meal | Roughly chop the remaining chestnuts

Spoon the sun-dried tomato oil into the skillet and put the pan over medium heat | Add the shallots and fry for 5 minutes, until soft | Add the sun-dried tomatoes and garlic and stir for 1 minute | Add the carrots, celery, rosemary, thyme, and sage and stir for 4–5 minutes | Add the minced mushrooms to the pan, increase the heat to high, and cook for 10 minutes, until the mushrooms are well sweated | Pour in the red wine and cranberry sauce | Add the bay leaf | Simmer for 6–7 minutes, until most of the liquid has evaporated | Reduce the heat, add the ground nutmeg and cinnamon, and stir for 1 minute

Take the roasted mushrooms out of the oven, turn off the heat, and open the foil | Transfer the mushrooms to a plate and pour the cooking liquid into a mixing bowl | Add the breadcrumbs and nut meal and mix everything together with a spoon | Tip in the mushroom mixture, removing the bay leaf | Fold everything together to form a thick, textured dough | Leave to cool to room temperature

Lay one sheet of puff pastry on the baking sheet | Spread half the mushroom mixture lengthwise down the middle of the pastry | Use your hands to mold it into a flat rectangular shape, leaving at least 2 inches of pastry on each side | Place the roasted mushrooms along the top of the mixture in two neat rows | Layer the rest of the mixture over the top, encasing the mushrooms completely | Smooth and shape into a neat rectangular mound

Brush a little milk around the exposed pastry edge using a pastry brush or your finger | Lay the second pastry sheet over the filling and smooth it down well, ensuring there are no air bubbles | Seal the edges by pressing the pastry sheets together all the way around the filling with your fingers | Trim any excess pastry from the edges, making sure you leave a ½-inch crust around the base of the Crisscross | Use a fork to crimp all around the edges of the pastry to firmly seal the pastry

Take a sharp knife and score a crisscross pattern across the top of the whole Crisscross | Pierce a few air vents in the top of the pastry | If you're feeling creative, cut a few decorative shapes from the excess pastry and place them on top of your Crisscross | Place in the fridge for 20 minutes | Preheat the oven to 350°F

Take the Crisscross out of the fridge and put it in the hot oven | Bake for 25 minutes

Meanwhile, make a glaze by pouring the maple syrup and milk into a small dish and mixing together | Take the Crisscross out of the oven and brush it all over with the glaze | Place back in the oven and bake until golden brown and crispy, about 25 minutes | Remove from the oven

Cut into slices and serve immediately with all the trimmings

BRUSSELS SPROUTS WITH MAPLE MUSHROOMS

SERVES 4

7 oz mixed mushrooms
¼ cups olive oil
1 tbsp maple syrup
1 tsp smoked salt
½ tsp smoked paprika
½ tsp black pepper, plus a little extra
    for seasoning
¼ cup sliced almonds
1 lb Brussels sprouts
2 large shallots
2 fresh bay leaves
salt

Preheat oven to 350°F | Line 2 sheet pans | Large saucepan of boiling salted water over high heat | Skillet

Chop the mushrooms into ¼-inch-thick slices and spread over one of the sheet pans | Drizzle with 2 tablespoons of the olive oil and the maple syrup | Sprinkle with the smoked salt, smoked paprika, and pepper | Toss well to coat | Put the pan in the oven for 25 minutes, turning halfway

Meanwhile, spread the sliced almonds over the second sheet pan | Put the pan in the oven for 10 minutes | Remove and set aside to cool

Meanwhile, trim off any old outer leaves from the sprouts | Put the sprouts in the pan of boiling salted water and cook for 5–6 minutes | Drain and set aside

Peel and thinly slice the shallots | Put the skillet over medium heat and add the remaining 2 tablespoons olive oil | When the pan is hot, add the shallots with a pinch of salt and fry for 2–3 minutes, until soft | Add the bay leaves and drained sprouts | Take the mushroom lardons out of the oven and transfer to the skillet | Cook for 3–4 minutes

Tip the cooked sprouts and mushrooms into a bowl | Sprinkle with the toasted sliced almonds | Season to perfection and serve

BANGERS IN BLANKETS

MAKES 12

6 plant-based sausages
1 medium eggplant

FOR THE MARINADE
¼ cup olive oil
1½ tbsp maple syrup
½ tsp smoked salt
1½ tsp smoked paprika
½ tsp black pepper

Preheat oven to 375°F | Line a sheet pan | Microwavable plate, optional | At least 12 toothpicks

If your sausages are frozen, put them on a microwavable plate and cook on full for 90 seconds to defrost | Alternatively, defrost in the fridge overnight

Pour all the ingredients for the marinade into a bowl | Mix with a fork until the salt has dissolved

Peel and trim the eggplant, then cut it lengthwise into quarters | Cut each quarter into thin slices, roughly ⅛ inch thick (you will need 12 thin slices) | Save any leftovers for a different recipe, like our Big Breakfast Bagel on page 258 | Toss in the smoky oil and marinate for 5 minutes

Cut all the sausages in half across the middle | Trim the cut edges to match the round ends | Tightly wrap the sausages in the marinated eggplant slices, securing them with toothpicks | Lay them on the lined sheet pan | Put the pan in the oven and bake for 10 minutes | Baste the sausages with the juices in the pan and cook for another 5 minutes | Baste again and cook for another 10 minutes | Baste once more and cook for another 5 minutes | Turn up the heat and give them a final blast for 5 minutes | Take out of the oven and serve immediately

CLEMENTINE ROASTED ROOT VEGETABLES

SERVES 4 AS A SIDE

1 lb heirloom carrots
4 medium beets
2 tbsp olive oil
2 tbsp water
1 tsp sea salt, plus a little extra
    for seasoning
2 clementines
2 tbsp balsamic vinegar
1 tbsp pomegranate molasses
½ oz fresh thyme
1 bay leaf
3½ oz walnuts
black pepper

Preheat oven to 375°F | Foil | 2 sheet pans | Roasting pan

Trim the carrots, peel them if the skins are tough, and cut any large ones in half lengthwise

Trim the beets, peel if desired, and cut them in half

Lay a large sheet of foil on a sheet pan | Place the beets in the middle and drizzle with 1 tablespoon of the olive oil, the water, and a little salt and pepper | Turn the beets to coat | Scrunch up the foil to make a package, making sure there are no gaps to let out any steam | Put the pan in the oven to steam for 1 hour

Meanwhile, put the carrots in the roasting pan | Zest one of the clementines over the carrots, then cut it in half horizontally and squeeze over the juice, catching any seeds in your other hand | Pour on the balsamic vinegar, pomegranate molasses, and the rest of the olive oil | Season with salt and pepper and stir to coat the carrots | Cut the remaining clementine in half horizontally and put it in the pan along with the thyme and bay leaf

When the beets have been in the oven for 30 minutes, put the carrots in and roast them for 25 minutes | Check if they are cooked and if they're still hard, return the pan to the oven for up to 10 minutes more

Put the walnuts on the second sheet pan | 10 minutes before the beets are ready to come out of the oven, put the walnuts in and bake, checking after 8 minutes to make sure they're not burning | Take the pan out of the oven, transfer the nuts to a cutting board, leave to cool slightly, and then roughly chop

Take the beets out of the oven and put the pan on a heatproof surface | Open the foil, leave to cool a little, then cut the beets into wedges

Remove the roasting pan from the oven | Tip in the beet wedges and toasted walnuts and stir them around in the caramelized carrot juices | Decorate with the roasted clementine and serve immediately

CRISPY, FLUFFY, PERFECT ROAST POTATOES

SERVES 4—6

3 lb 5 oz russet potatoes
3 tbsp salt
¼ cup olive oil
1 garlic bulb
2 sprigs fresh sage
10 sprigs fresh thyme
4 sprigs fresh rosemary

Preheat oven to 425°F | Half fill a large bowl with cold water | Large saucepan | Large sheet pan | Line 2 plates with paper towels

Peel the potatoes and place them in the bowl of cold water to get rid of the excess starch | Drain and tip into the saucepan | Cover with cold water | Add half the salt | Put the pan over high heat and bring to a boil | Boil for 8 minutes | Tip the potatoes into a colander and leave to steam dry for 5 minutes

Shake the potatoes in the colander to rough the edges (this will give you a perfect, crunchy crust) | Spread the potatoes over the sheet pan so that they're not touching | Pour on the olive oil and sprinkle with the remaining salt | Turn the potatoes to make sure they're well coated

Put the pan in the oven and roast the potatoes for 30 minutes | Break the garlic bulb into separate cloves | Remove the potatoes from the oven and add the garlic, sage, thyme, and rosemary sprigs | Turn the potatoes again to coat | Put the pan back in the oven and roast for 40–50 minutes longer, until the skins are incredibly crispy and a deep golden color

Take the pan out of the oven | Transfer the potatoes to the plates covered with paper towels to drain the excess oil | Serve with a full roast and all the trimmings!

ULTIMATE ROAST STUFFING BALLS

MAKES 16

1 oz walnuts
1 small onion
1 parsnip (about 5 oz)
1 ripe Bosc pear
7 oz whole wheat bread
½ oz fresh sage
1 tbsp olive oil, plus extra for greasing
1 oz dried cranberries
⅛ tsp ground allspice
⅛ tsp ground nutmeg
½ cup unsweetened plant-based milk

Preheat oven to 350°F | Line a sheet pan | Food processor | Medium saucepan

Spread the walnuts over the sheet pan | Put the pan in the oven for 8–9 minutes, until the nuts are lightly toasted | Remove, transfer to a cutting board, and roughly chop

Peel and finely dice the onion, parsnip, and pear | Remove and discard the crusts from the bread, then blitz the bread to make breadcrumbs | Roughly chop the sage

Place the saucepan over medium heat and add the oil | Add the onion and fry for 5–6 minutes, stirring, until soft and translucent | Add the parsnip and pears, stir, and cook for 6–7 minutes | Add half the breadcrumbs to the pan and stir for 3–4 minutes until they start to turn golden | Take the pan off the heat and tip the contents into a large bowl

Add the sage, walnuts, dried cranberries, allspice, nutmeg, plant-based milk, and remaining breadcrumbs to the bowl and mix well to bring the ingredients together

Lightly oil the lined sheet pan you used before | Use your hands to roll 16 walnut-sized balls of stuffing and place them on the pan | Put them in the oven and bake for 35–40 minutes until golden and firm to the touch | Remove from the oven and serve

PERFECT GRAVY

MAKES ABOUT 3⅓ CUPS

1 large onion
2 carrots (about 12 oz)
1 leek
2 celery stalks
4 garlic cloves
1 bay leaf
a small bunch of fresh thyme
1 sprig fresh rosemary
3 tbsp olive oil
2 tsp salt
1 tsp black pepper
1¾ oz dried porcini mushrooms
2½ tbsp flour
¼ cup water
2 cups vegetable stock
1 tbsp soy sauce
7 tbsp port

Preheat oven to 375°F | Large roasting pan | Boiling water | Potato masher or stick blender | 2 large saucepans

First roast the vegetables | Peel and quarter the onion | Trim the carrots, leek, and celery and cut them into 1½–2-inch pieces | Put all the vegetables into the roasting pan along with the unpeeled garlic cloves, bay leaf, thyme, and rosemary | Drizzle with the olive oil and sprinkle with the salt and pepper | Place in the oven and roast for 45 minutes, tossing once halfway through

Put the porcini mushrooms into a mug and fill it with boiling water | Leave to soak while the vegetables roast

Take the vegetables out of the oven | Peel the skins off the garlic cloves, then mash all the vegetables in the pan with a potato masher or pulse with a stick blender until mushy but not smooth | Transfer to one of the large saucepans

Put the flour into a mug and add the water | Whisk with a fork until all the lumps have dissolved | Add to the saucepan | Pour in the porcini mushrooms and soaking liquid | Add the vegetable stock, soy sauce, and port | Place over high heat | Stir continuously until the gravy is bubbling, then reduce the heat and simmer for about 30 minutes, checking regularly to ensure it doesn't stick to the pan

When the gravy reaches your ideal thickness, pour it through a sieve into the second pan, forcing the gravy through with a wooden spoon | Put the pan over very low heat to keep warm until you are ready to serve, then transfer to a serving jug or gravy boat

SHARING COCKTAIL PITCHERS

It'll be no surprise to you that we enjoy a cocktail from time to time, but making them yourself at home does involve a fair bit of work. A cocktail pitcher is a much more efficient way to enjoy a tasty drink with friends! With the exception of the mango lassi, all of these drinks lend themselves really well to different fruity flavors, so try varying the fruit or berries in the agua fresca, sangria, or daiquiri for a whole lot more cocktail fun.

STRAWBERRY DAIQUIRI SLUSHY

SERVES 4

Blender | 1-quart pitcher

1 lb strawberries, frozen if possible
4 limes
6 tbsp agave syrup
1 cup white rum
¾ oz fresh mint
ice

Hull the strawberries, if fresh, spread over a baking sheet, and put in the freezer for at least 2 hours or ideally overnight

Cut all the limes in half and squeeze the juice into the blender | Add the syrup, frozen strawberries, and rum and blend until liquid | Fill the blender to the top with ice and pulse until you've reach a slushy consistency | Pour the daiquiri into a pitcher, add the mint, and serve immediately

NAUGHTY AGUA FRESCA

SERVES 4

Blender | 1-quart pitcher

1 lb 5 oz strawberries
1 small pineapple (about 2 lb 13 oz unpeeled weight)
1 tbsp superfine sugar
7 tbsp vodka
7 tbsp cold water
ice

Hull the strawberries | Peel and core the pineapple and chop it into chunks | Put the fruit, sugar, vodka, and water into the blender and blend until liquid | Fill a quarter of the pitcher with ice and pour in the agua fresca | Serve immediately

CHEEKY MANGO LASSI

SERVES 4

Blender | 1-quart pitcher

4 ripe mangoes
16 oz dairy-free yogurt
2–4 tbsp agave syrup
2 limes
7 tbsp white rum
ice

Slice the mangoes lengthwise down either side of the stone | Spoon the flesh into the blender and blend to a purée | Add the dairy-free yogurt and agave syrup | Zest both the limes into the blender, then cut them in half and squeeze in the juice | Add the rum | Blend until completely smooth | Fill a quarter of the jug with ice and pour over the lassi | Serve immediately

FRUITY SANGRIA

SERVES 4

1-quart pitcher

7 oz strawberries
1 orange
2 ripe peaches
3 tbsp brown sugar
3 cups Spanish red wine
generous ¾ cups orange juice
3 tbsp brandy
a little sparkling water, optional
a small bunch of mint
ice

Hull the strawberries and cut them in half | Cut the orange into slices | Cut the peaches in half, cut out the pits, and slice | Put all the fruit into the pitcher | Sprinkle with the brown sugar | Pour in the red wine, orange juice, and brandy | Taste and add a little sparkling water or extra brandy if you like | Put the bunch of mint in the pitcher and fill it to the top with ice | Stir everything together with a long wooden spoon and serve immediately

Pictured on pages 146—147

STRAWBERRY
DAIQUIRI SLUSHY

NAUGHTY AGUA
FRESCA

CHEEKY MANGO
LASSI

FRUITY SANGRIA

SIDES & SHARERS

Henry's favorite
Party Poppers with BOSH! BBQ Sauce

Ian's favorite
Wild West Wings

CAMEMBOSH HEDGEHOG

This always generates big smiles in all who behold it! Big thanks to Ellie from Kinda Co (makers of incredible plant-based cheeses) for the original recipe, which we collaborated on together in the early days of BOSH! Tapioca flour is crucial for optimum gooeyness, so do seek some out. To get ahead, make the cheese the day before and keep it in the fridge.

SERVES 6

2½ oz cashews
1 (14 oz) Tiger loaf (aka Dutch Crunch or Marco Polo bread)
2 garlic cloves
1 tbsp tapioca flour
1½ tsp salt, plus extra for seasoning
1 tbsp nutritional yeast
1 tsp apple cider vinegar
⅔ cup warm water
1 sprig fresh rosemary
1 tsp olive oil
black pepper

FOR THE HERB OIL
2 garlic cloves
1 sprig fresh rosemary
1 tsp salt
¼ tsp black pepper
½ cup olive oil

Preheat oven to 350°F | Line a baking sheet | Line a 5-inch round ovenproof dish with parchment paper | Small saucepan of boiling water over medium heat | Pestle and mortar, optional | Blender | Boiling water

···

First make the cheese | Add the cashews to the pan of hot water and boil for 20 minutes to soften | Remove from the heat, drain, and leave to cool

Prepare the loaf | Use a bread knife to cut even slices across the top of the loaf, 1¼ inches apart, making sure you don't cut all the way through as the base needs to remain intact | Turn the loaf 90 degrees and cut across the first slices to make a crisscross pattern

To make the herb oil, peel and roughly chop the garlic | Remove the leaves from the rosemary by running your thumb and forefinger from the top to the base of the stem (the leaves should easily come away) and finely chop | Put the garlic, rosemary, salt, and pepper into the mortar and bash them with the pestle to make a paste (or put the ingredients in a small bowl and use the end of a rolling pin) | Pour the olive oil into the mortar and mix with a fork

Put the loaf on the baking sheet | Use a pastry brush or teaspoon to drizzle the herb oil deep inside the cuts | Put the baking sheet in the oven and cook for 25–30 minutes, until golden and toasted

Meanwhile, finish the cheese | Peel 1 of the garlic cloves and put it in the blender | Add the drained cashews, tapioca flour, salt, nutritional yeast, apple cider vinegar, and warm water | Blend to a smooth cream

Pour the cashew cream into the saucepan, taste, and season with salt and pepper | Put the saucepan over medium heat and cook, stirring constantly, for 2 minutes, until slightly thickened | Pour into the parchment-lined dish

Peel the remaining garlic clove and cut it into sticks | Remove the rosemary needles | Gently push the garlic sticks and rosemary needles into the top of the cashew cheese so that they stick out the top | Drizzle over the olive oil and sprinkle over a little black pepper

When ready to serve, put the cashew cheese in the oven alongside the bread and bake for the final 12–15 minutes, until the cheese has formed a skin and the color has darkened | Remove and serve immediately

SUSHI CUPCAKES

This is a fun take on sushi! This fantastic technique allows you to exercise your creativity and create food that's tasty, healthy, and truly Instagram-worthy. Tag us in your photos with #sushicupcakes. We put hoisin sauce in the middle of our cupcakes, but you can add whatever you like. Wasabi and ginger is a great traditional filling.

MAKES 12

2 cups sushi rice
2 tbsp rice vinegar
2 tbsp superfine sugar
½ tsp salt
12 nori sheets
2 tbsp hoisin sauce
pickled ginger, for serving
black sesame seeds, for sprinkling
soy sauce, for serving
wasabi, to serve, optional

FOR THE VEGETABLE TOPPINGS
1 red bell pepper
1 carrot
¼ cucumber
1 small avocado
10 fresh chives
5 radishes

FOR THE DIPPING SAUCE
sriracha
egg-free mayonnaise

Small saucepan | Grease a sheet pan with neutral oil (such as vegetable or sunflower) | 5½-inch saucer | Ruler, optional | 12-cup (or 2 x 6-cup) muffin tin

Cook the sushi rice following the instructions on the package, ensuring that it is dry and sticky when cooked

Put the saucepan over medium heat | Pour in the rice vinegar, sugar, and salt and heat until the sugar has dissolved | Let cool to room temperature, then pour over the cooked rice, gently stirring until all the liquid is absorbed | Spread the rice over the greased sheet pan and let cool to room temperature, when it should be dry but sticky

Stack the nori sheets and lay the saucer on top | Cut around it to make nori rounds | Find the center of the nori stack and cut a neat, straight slit from the center to the outer edges | Take one round and fashion a cone that is roughly 3 inches wide at the top | Wet your finger and lightly brush along the slit to stick it in place | Put the cone in one of the muffin cups | Repeat to fill all the muffin cups

Wet your hands and roll a golf ball-sized ball of rice | Poke a hole in the center and pour in ½ teaspoon hoisin sauce | Pack more rice over the hole to seal in the sauce | Smooth the outside and place in one of the nori muffin cases | Repeat to fill all the cases

Get all your toppings ready | Cut the bell pepper in half, cut out the stems and seeds, and thinly slice | Peel the carrot and cut into matchsticks, thin rounds, or ribbons | Cut the cucumber in the same way | Halve and carefully pit the avocado by tapping the pit firmly with the heel of a knife so that it lodges in the pit, then twist and remove, then finely slice | Chop the chives | Trim and thinly slice the radishes

Make a quick dipping sauce by stirring sriracha into the egg-free mayonnaise to taste | Finely chop the pickled ginger

Decorate your sushi cupcakes with the prepared vegetables and sprinkle them with black sesame seeds | Serve with soy sauce, wasabi, if using, pickled ginger, and the dipping sauce on the side

LOADED POTATO NACHOS

This dish is perfect movie night fodder. Try it with sweet potatoes too—just keep an eye on them to get the right crispiness. The sour cream and salsa will keep in the fridge for up to 3 days, but the guac should be eaten the day you make it—it keeps in the fridge for a few hours if you squeeze a good amount of lemon juice over the top and cover the bowl.

SERVES 4

6 tbsp olive oil
1½ tbsp garlic powder
1½ tbsp onion powder
1 tbsp paprika
2 tsp cayenne pepper
2 tsp salt
1 tsp black pepper
1½ lb russet potatoes
7 oz cherry tomatoes
3½ oz dairy-free pizza cheese
scant ½ cup pickled jalapeños
1 (14 oz) can refried beans

FOR THE TOPPINGS

Sour Cream (store-bought or see opposite)
Salsa (store-bought or see opposite)
Green Chili Guacamole (store-bought or see opposite)
½ cup cilantro leaves, optional

Preheat oven to 350°F | Grater | Blender | Large mixing bowl | Line 3 baking sheets | Lasagna pan | Foil

First cover the potatoes in a spicy coating | Put the olive oil, garlic powder, onion powder, paprika, cayenne pepper, salt, and pepper into a bowl and mix with a fork | Cut the potatoes into slices a scant ⅛ inch thick and add them to the bowl | Toss to coat evenly in the flavored oil

Spread the potato slices over the baking sheets | Put the sheets in the oven and bake for 20 minutes, until golden brown, swapping the sheets between the racks halfway through to ensure even cooking | Remove from the oven and set aside to cool to room temperature

While the potatoes are cooking and cooling, get your fillings and toppings ready | Finely chop the cherry tomatoes | Grate the dairy-free cheese | Finely chop the jalapeños | Make the sour cream, salsa, and guacamole (see opposite)

Now layer up the nachos | Cover the bottom of the lasagna pan with potato slices | Spread over some refried beans, cherry tomatoes, jalapeños, and dairy-free cheese | Repeat to layer up the dish, finishing with a layer of potatoes and light sprinkling of cheese | Cover with foil, then pierce it a few times with a fork | Put the dish in the oven and bake for 20 minutes, removing the foil halfway through, until the nachos around the edges of the dish are crisping up

When the nachos are cooked, drizzle with the sour cream | Spoon on the salsa | Dollop with the guacamole | Sprinkle on the cilantro leaves, if using, and serve immediately

Pictured on pages 156–157

SOUR CREAM

SERVES 4

½ lemon
7 oz cashews
2 tsp nutritional yeast
½ tsp salt
½ cup water

Blender

Squeeze the lemon juice into the blender, catching any seeds in your other hand | Add all the rest of the ingredients | Blend to a very smooth cream | Taste, season with more salt, and loosen with a little water if necessary to reach your desired consistency and serve, or refrigerate until needed

QUICK SALSA

SERVES 4

4 large tomatoes
4 scallions
½ oz cilantro
1 tbsp pickled jalapeños
1 lime
1 small garlic clove
¾ tsp salt

Fine grater or Microplane

Finely chop the tomatoes | Thinly slice the scallions | Pick the leaves from the cilantro and chop roughly | Chop the pickled jalapeños | Cut the lime in half | Peel and grate the garlic

Squeeze the lime juice into a bowl | Add all the rest of the salsa ingredients and mix together | Pour into a sieve and leave to drain for 2–3 minutes | Tip the salsa back into the bowl and serve, or cover and refrigerate until needed

GREEN CHILI GUACAMOLE

SERVES 4

3 ripe avocados
4 cherry tomatoes
½ small red onion
1 small garlic clove
1 fresh green chili
1 lime
½ lemon
½ tsp salt

Fine grater or Microplane

Halve and carefully pit the avocados by tapping the pit firmly with the heel of a knife so that it lodges in the pit, then twist and remove | Scoop out the flesh | Finely chop the tomatoes | Peel and mince the red onion | Peel and finely grate the garlic | Rip the stem from the chili and chop finely | Put all the prepared ingredients into a large bowl | Cut the lime in half and squeeze in the juice | Squeeze in the lemon juice, catching any seeds with your other hand | Mash well with a fork until really creamy | Taste, season with salt, and serve or cover and refrigerate until needed

SATAY SUMMER ROLLS

There's something so satisfying about making your own summer rolls. It's a little fiddly, but once you've done a couple you'll be in the swing of things. The satay sauce goes really well with Thai crackers or on the side of any Thai meal, so make a batch and keep it in the fridge for up to 2 days. The rolls make an excellent packed lunch too. You'll be the envy of your friends!

MAKES 16

3½ oz dried rice vermicelli
1 large carrot
½ cucumber
3½ oz red cabbage
a small bunch of fresh mint
a small bunch of cilantro
a small bunch of fresh Thai basil
a small handful of fresh chives
a small handful of salted roasted peanuts
16 rice paper wrappers

FOR THE CRISPY TOFU
1 (10 oz) block extra-firm tofu
3 tbsp cornstarch
3 tbsp sesame oil

FOR THE DRESSING
1 lime
1 fresh red chili
¾-inch piece fresh ginger
1 tsp superfine sugar
1 tsp soy sauce
½ tbsp rice vinegar

FOR THE SATAY DIPPING SAUCE
2 limes
1 bird's-eye chili
1 garlic clove
6 tbsp crunchy peanut butter
2 tbsp brown sugar
1 tbsp soy sauce

Tofu press or 2 clean kitchen towels and a weight such as a heavy book | Medium saucepan | Skillet | Line a plate with paper towels | Fine grater or Microplane

Press the tofu using a tofu press or place it between two clean kitchen towels, lay it on a plate, and put a weight on top | Leave for at least 30 minutes to drain and firm up before you start cooking

Cook the vermicelli following the instructions on the package | Rinse, drain thoroughly, then tip into a bowl

Cut the tofu into 16 strips about a scant ¼ inch wide | Put the cornstarch into a dish | Add the tofu strips and toss to coat | Place the skillet over high heat | Pour in the oil and let it get very hot | Add the tofu strips in batches and fry until crisp and golden | Transfer to paper towels to drain

To make the dressing, zest the lime into a bowl, cut it in half, and squeeze in the juice | Rip the stem from the chile and finely chop | Peel the ginger by scraping off the skin with a spoon and grate it into the bowl | Add the sugar, soy sauce, and rice vinegar and mix

Prepare the rest of the fresh filling ingredients | Peel the carrot | Cut the carrot and cucumber into matchsticks | Trim and thinly slice the red cabbage | Put the veggies into a bowl and drizzle with 1 tablespoon of the dressing | Drizzle 1 tablespoon of dressing over the noodles

Pick the leaves from the herbs | Snip the chives into 4-inch lengths | Roughly chop the roasted peanuts

Now start making your summer rolls | Half fill a bowl with cold water | Submerge a rice wrapper until it is soft and pliable but not completely soggy | Lay on a cutting board | Arrange some herbs, sliced vegetables, a tofu strip, noodles, and chopped peanuts down the middle | Bring the bottom edge of the wrapper up over the filling, fold one side over and roll up tightly, then fold down the top to seal | Place on a plate, join-side down | Repeat to use up all the tofu strips

To make the satay dipping sauce, halve the limes and squeeze the juice into a bowl | Rip the stem from the chili and thinly slice | Peel and grate the garlic | Add all the ingredients to the bowl and mix well

Serve the fresh summer rolls with the dipping sauce on the side

WILD WEST WINGS

These wings are simply incredible. After a trip to LA we created this recipe inspired by a Gordon Ramsay video. Our talented foodie friend Clare Gray suggested we try oyster mushrooms instead of seitan, and our Wild West Wings were born! You can also try other mushrooms, such as shiitake. Our hot sauces are spectacular and keep in a jar in the fridge for up to 2 weeks.

SERVES 4

generous ¾ cup unsweetened plant-based milk

3½ oz coconut yogurt (the thicker the better)

1 tsp salt

1–2 lemons

1 lb oyster mushrooms

1⅓ cups all-purpose flour

½ tsp black pepper

2 tsp cayenne pepper

1 tsp smoked paprika

1 tsp garlic powder

fresh chives, to garnish

1 fresh red chili, for garnish

vegetable oil, for frying

Whisk | 2 large mixing bowls | Large saucepan | Cooking thermometer, optional | Paper towels

· ·

First make the marinade for the mushrooms | Put the milk, coconut yogurt, and salt in a large mixing bowl | Slice the lemons and squeeze in the juice reasonably sparingly, catching any seeds in your other hand | The batter shouldn't be too thin | Whisk until there are no lumps | Add the mushrooms and stir to coat | Leave for 10 minutes to marinate

To make a dry coating, put the flour, pepper, cayenne pepper, smoked paprika, and garlic powder in the second mixing bowl and mix together with a fork

If you're making your own hot sauce (see opposite), make it now and set it to one side

Pour oil into the saucepan to a depth of 3 inches and heat to 350°F, or until a wooden spoon dipped into the oil sizzles around the edges | Pick the mushrooms out of the marinade and transfer them to the bowl of dry ingredients | Toss until really well coated

Place the mushrooms in the pan, in batches, making sure not to overcrowd the pan | Cook for 4–5 minutes, turning regularly, until deep golden brown | Transfer to the paper towels with a slotted spoon for 2 minutes to soak up the excess oil

Place the wings on a serving platter | Drizzle with some hot sauce and serve the rest in a bowl for dipping | Finely chop the chives and sprinkle over | Rip the stem from the chili, cut it in half lengthwise, and remove the seeds if you prefer, then finely chop and scatter over the Wild West Wings

Pictured on pages 162–63

DE LA SEOUL HOT SAUCE

MAKES ABOUT ⅔ CUP

Fine grater or Microplane | Small pan

....

2 large garlic cloves
¾-inch piece fresh ginger
1 tbsp sesame oil
3 tbsp maple syrup
1 tbsp soy sauce
3 tbsp sriracha

Peel and grate the garlic | Peel the ginger by scraping off the skin with a spoon and grate | Put the small pan over medium heat and pour in the sesame oil | Add the garlic and ginger and cook for 3 minutes, until starting to soften | Pour into a dish and add the maple syrup, soy sauce, and sriracha | Stir everything together well

WILD WEST HOT SAUCE

MAKES ABOUT ⅔ CUP

Blender

....

5 mixed chilies (we used fresh red chilies,
    1 Thai chili, and 1 Scotch bonnet)
1 red bell pepper
3 garlic cloves
1 lime
2 roasted red peppers in oil (from a jar)
3 tbsp + 1 tsp superfine sugar
1 tbsp cornstarch or all-purpose flour
½ tsp salt
3 tbsp white wine vinegar

Rip the stems from the chilies, cut them in half lengthwise, and remove the seeds if you prefer a milder sauce | Cut the bell pepper in half and cut out the stem and seeds, then roughly chop | Peel the garlic cloves | Cut the lime in half and squeeze the juice into the blender | Add all the remaining ingredients and blend to a smooth paste

WILD WEST
HOT SAUCE

DE LA SEOUL
HOT SAUCE

PARTY POPPERS WITH BOSH! BBQ SAUCE

These popcorn bites are fried twice for incredible crispiness. It's quite a long recipe, so double it and freeze half the poppers after their first fry for up to a month. You can make this quicker by frying just once at 350°F and skipping the extra steps. But those extra steps are definitely worth it!

SERVES 4 AS A SIDE

FOR THE PARTY POPPERS
3 oz vital wheat gluten
2 tbsp nutritional yeast
½ tsp onion powder
½ tsp garlic powder
¼ tsp ground sage
¼ tsp ground thyme
½ tsp sea salt, plus extra for sprinkling
½ tsp black pepper
½ tsp ground cumin
generous ½ cup vegetable stock
1½ tbsp olive oil
½ tsp apple cider vinegar
½–¾ cup cilantro leaves
½ tbsp chili flakes
¼ cup BBQ sauce, store-bought or use our recipe on page 166, or store-bought teriyaki sauce, for serving
vegetable oil, for deep-frying

FOR THE BUTTERMILK MARINADE
2 lemons
1⅔ cups unsweetened soy milk
7 oz coconut yogurt (the thicker the better)
2 tsp salt

FOR THE DRY COATING
2⅓ cups all-purpose flour, plus extra for dusting
2 tsp cayenne pepper
2 tsp smoked paprika
2 tsp garlic powder
1 tsp black pepper

Clean work surface dusted liberally with flour | Large saucepan with a lid | Boiling water | Steamer basket or colander | Large deep-sided skillet | Cooking thermometer | Line a large plate with paper towels | Clear some space in the freezer | Freezer bags

First make the dough for the poppers | Place the vital wheat gluten, nutritional yeast, and all the herbs and spices in a large bowl and mix to combine | In a separate bowl or measuring cup, mix together the vegetable stock, olive oil, and apple cider vinegar | Pour the wet ingredients into the dry ingredients and mix thoroughly until it comes together as a dough

Tip the dough onto the floured work surface and knead for 10 minutes, until the dough becomes uniform and a bit spongy, being careful not to overwork it as it can get tough | Cut into ⅓-inch cubes

Put the large saucepan over medium-high heat | Pour boiling water into the saucepan until it's ¾ inch deep | Place the steamer basket or colander on top of the pan and add the dough cubes | Cover with the lid and simmer for 45 minutes to steam the dough | Check the water every now and then and top it up with boiling water if necessary to stop the pan burning dry | Remove after 45 minutes and set aside to cool to room temperature

To make the buttermilk marinade, cut the lemons in half and squeeze the juice into a bowl, catching any seeds in your other hand | Pour in the soy milk, coconut yogurt, and salt | Whisk together well

Now make the dry coating by combining all the ingredients in a separate bowl

Put the cooled dough cubes into the buttermilk marinade and stir to cover | Leave for 10 minutes to marinate

Dip the marinated dough pieces into the dry batter, rolling them around to coat | Now double-dip them in the marinade and roll them in the dry batter for a second time

Continued on next page

For the first fry, pour vegetable oil for deep-frying into the large skillet so that it comes no more than halfway up the sides | Heat the oil to 265°F (this is a fairly low temperature for deep-frying so if you don't have a thermometer, drop a cube of bread into the pan to test the temperature: when it's ready it should float but take a little while to brown) | Transfer some of the battered poppers to the pan using a slotted spoon—do this in batches so the oil stays at the correct temperature | Fry, turning regularly, until light golden brown and a light crust has started to form, about 3 minutes | Transfer to the plate lined with paper towels to drain and cool to room temperature, then transfer to freezer bags and put them in the freezer for at least an hour | Keep the oil in the pan to use again later

Once the bites are frozen, take them out of the freezer | Reheat the oil to 350°F, or until a wooden spoon dipped into the oil sizzles around the edges | Fry in batches, for about 5 minutes, until dark golden brown | Transfer to paper towels and sprinkle with sea salt

Finely chop the cilantro leaves and sprinkle over the poppers along with the chili flakes | Serve with BBQ sauce or your favorite dip on the side

BOSH! BBQ SAUCE

MAKES ABOUT 9 oz

1 tbsp vegetable oil
2 small onions
2 fresh red chilies
1½-inch piece fresh ginger
4 garlic cloves
1¼ cups apple juice
generous ¾ cup red wine vinegar
⅔ cup soy sauce
¼ cup tomato ketchup
2 tbsp Dijon mustard
1 cup light brown sugar

Medium saucepan over medium heat | Sterilized bottle or jar (see page 39)

Add the oil to the pan | Peel and finely chop the onions and add them to the pan | Cook for 5 minutes, stirring

Rip the stems from the chilies, cut them in half lengthwise, and remove the seeds if you prefer a milder sauce, then finely chop | Peel the ginger by scraping off the skin with a spoon and finely chop | Peel and finely chop the garlic

Add all of the ingredients to the pan and stir until the sugar dissolves | Bring to a boil, then reduce the heat to a low simmer | Cook for 40–45 minutes, until the sauce is thick and you have about 1 cup | Taste and season | Use it just as it is or for a more typical, smooth sauce, blend in a blender until smooth | Transfer to a sterilized bottle or jar and store in the fridge

BIG BAD BHAJIS WITH SPICY TOMATO CHUTNEY

The ubiquitous Indian snack, the bhaji, gets the BOSH! treatment with the addition of fenugreek seeds and a winner of a chutney. Bhajis are a great way of using up leftover veg—try adding finely match-sticked eggplant, potato, scallions, or broccolini to the mix. Taste the batter as you go and adjust to your preferences.

MAKES 8

2 large white onions
1 garlic clove
2-inch piece fresh ginger
1 fresh red chili
¾ oz cilantro
2½ cups chickpea flour
⅔ cup sweetcorn kernels
1 tbsp nigella seeds
1 tbsp ground coriander
1 tbsp ground cumin
1 tbsp salt
1 tbsp garam masala
1 tsp ground fenugreek, optional
1 tsp ground turmeric
generous ¾ cup water
vegetable oil, for deep-frying

FOR THE SPICY TOMATO CHUTNEY
2 tbsp vegetable oil
½ tsp fenugreek seeds, optional
1 tsp nigella seeds
1 tsp cumin seeds
1 tsp black mustard seeds
1 tsp fennel seeds
2-inch piece fresh ginger
1 (14.5 oz) can diced tomatoes
6 tbsp superfine sugar
1 tsp salt
1 tbsp chili flakes

Large saucepan over medium heat | Line a large plate with paper towels | Fine grater or Microplane

First make the chutney | Pour the oil into the pan and let it heat up | Add the fenugreek seeds, if using | Add the nigella, cumin, black mustard, and fennel seeds and fry until the seeds are aromatic and starting to crackle | Peel the ginger by scraping off the skin with a spoon, then grate it into the pan | Stir for 1 minute | Pour in the diced tomatoes and heat for 2–3 minutes until simmering | Add the sugar and salt and stir until the sugar dissolves | Turn down the heat and let everything simmer gently, stirring occasionally, for 10–12 minutes, until thick and syrupy | Stir in the chili flakes | Pour the chutney into a heatproof serving dish and leave to cool to room temperature | Clean out the pan

To make the bhajis, peel and thinly slice the onions | Peel and grate the garlic | Peel the ginger by scraping off the skin with a spoon, then finely grate it | Rip the stem from the chili, cut it in half lengthwise, and remove the seeds if you prefer a milder flavor, then thinly slice | Rip the leaves from the cilantro and discard the stems | Put all the bhaji ingredients except for the oil into a bowl | Mix everything together to form a thick, textured batter

Put the clean saucepan back over medium heat | Pour in the vegetable oil until it's 4–4¾ inches deep | Heat until a wooden spoon dipped into the oil sizzles around the edges

Roll a golf-ball-sized piece of batter in your hands | Carefully squash the ball so that it's about ¾ inch thick | Repeat to use up all the bhaji batter | Carefully place a few bhajis in the oil and fry for 3–4 minutes, until golden and crispy | Transfer to the plate lined with paper towels using a slotted spoon | Repeat to cook all the bhajis | Serve immediately with the spicy tomato chutney

BBQ BEANS WITH MUSHROOM BURNT ENDS

We love this recipe. Homemade baked beans are so easy yet feel like such a treat! The burnt ends give the whole dish a wonderfully smoky flavor. We also suggest pairing this with our Sheet-Pan Breakfast (see page 270) for the ultimate cooked breakfast.

SERVES 1–2

½ onion
2 garlic cloves
1 tbsp olive oil
1 tbsp tomato paste
¼ tsp smoked paprika
¼ tsp chili powder
¼ tsp dried thyme
1 tbsp light brown sugar
1 tbsp reduced-sodium soy sauce
1 (14 oz) can cannellini beans
¾ cup tomato puree
salt and black pepper

FOR THE MUSHROOM BURNT ENDS
7 oz mixed mushrooms
1 tbsp olive oil
3 tbsp good-quality BBQ sauce
salt

Large skillet | Medium saucepan

First make the burnt ends | Thinly slice the mushrooms | Add the tablespoon of olive oil to the skillet and place over medium-high heat | Add the mushrooms | Sprinkle with a good pinch of salt | Fry, stirring regularly, until very browned but not burnt, about 10 minutes | Add the BBQ sauce to the pan and stir to coat | Cook for another 1–3 minutes, until the sauce has fully coated and caramelized around the mushrooms and the mushrooms have blackened (but are not burnt)

Meanwhile, make the BBQ beans | Peel and finely chop the onion and garlic | Add the tablespoon of olive oil to the saucepan and place over medium heat | Add the onion and sauté for 5 minutes | Add the garlic and sauté for 3 minutes | Add the tomato paste, smoked paprika, chili powder, thyme, sugar, and soy sauce and stir them into the onions | Cook for 2 minutes longer

Drain and rinse the cannellini beans, then add them to the pan and stir | Cook for another 2–3 minutes | Pour in the tomato puree and let it simmer until the sauce has thickened, about 5 minutes | Taste and season

Serve up the beans and spoon the mushroom burnt ends on top, stirring some into the beans

NOTTING HILL PATTIES

These patties are perfect for a summer party or BBQ! They go great with West Indian–style hot sauce (Encona) or with our sauce on page 166. This recipe makes enough for six awesome little patties, and one or two should easily be enough for a delicious lunch on the go, so wrap 'em up in foil and take them with you!

MAKES 6

8 tbsp dairy-free butter
1¾ cups all-purpose flour, plus extra for dusting
1 tsp ground turmeric
¼ tsp salt
2–3 tbsp water
unsweetened plant-based milk, for brushing

FOR THE FILLING
6 plant-based sausages
2 garlic cloves
1¼-inch piece fresh ginger
5 scallions
4 medium tomatoes
2 sprigs fresh thyme
2 tbsp olive oil
1 tbsp soy sauce
¼ tsp ground allspice
½ tsp black pepper
2 tsp West Indian–style hot sauce (Encona), plus a little extra
1 tsp ketchup

Preheat oven to 390°F | Line a sheet pan | Microwavable plate, optional | Fine grater or Microplane | Large skillet | Rolling pin or clean, dry wine bottle | Pastry brush

....

Put your sausages on a microwavable plate and put the plate in the microwave | If they are frozen, cook on high for 90 seconds; if they're not frozen, cook for 20 seconds | Take out of the microwave and mash with a fork | Alternatively, defrost the sausages in the fridge overnight, put them in the oven for 5 minutes, and mash with a fork

Peel and grate the garlic | Peel the ginger by scraping off the skin with a spoon, then grate | Thinly slice the scallions | Finely chop the tomatoes | Remove the leaves from the thyme if the stem is woody, then chop finely

Place the skillet over medium heat and add the oil | Add the minced sausage and fry, stirring constantly, for 4–5 minutes, until beginning to color | Add the scallions and stir for 2 minutes | Add the garlic and ginger and stir for 2 minutes | Add the soy sauce, thyme, allspice, black pepper, hot sauce, and ketchup and stir for 2 minutes | Pour the tomatoes into the pan and stir for 2–3 minutes, until half the liquid has evaporated | Take off the heat and leave to cool to room temperature

Put the dairy-free butter into a mixing bowl and sprinkle with the flour, turmeric, and salt | Rub between your fingers to make a dry, crumbly mixture | Add the water and work it into the butter mixture with your fingers to make a dough

Divide the dough into 6 equal pieces, about 2 oz each | Dust a clean work surface with flour | Roll the dough pieces into thin ovals about 8 inches long, 6 inches wide, and ⅛ inch thick | Spoon the filling into the center of each pastry oval | Brush around the edges with water and fold over lengthwise | Crimp around the edges with a fork to seal and prick holes in the tops with a fork | Put on the baking sheet and refrigerate for 15 minutes

Take the sheet out of the fridge | Brush the patties lightly with plant-based milk

Put the sheet in the oven and bake for 20 minutes, until firm to the touch | Leave to cool slightly, then serve

TEXAN POTATO SALAD

This deliciously satisfying salad was the brainchild of our friend Sophie Pryn when she whipped up a deliciously fresh accompaniment to our Wild West Wings on page 160. It's great the next day too, so pack any leftovers into a lunchbox. You can replace the potatoes with sweet potatoes; just cook them for a bit less time.

SERVES 6–8

2 lb new potatoes
2 celery stalks
1 red bell pepper
8 scallions
8 small gherkins pickles
¼ cup capers
1 lemon
½ oz fresh dill
½ oz fresh parsley
½ oz fresh mint
½ oz cilantro
generous ½ cup egg-free mayonnaise
¾ tsp salt, plus extra

Large saucepan

Put the potatoes in the pan, fill it with water, and sprinkle in a generous pinch of salt | Turn the heat to high, bring to a boil, and cook for 15–20 minutes, until tender

Prep the rest of the veg | Thinly slice the celery | Cut the bell pepper in half, cut out the stem and seeds, and dice the flesh | Trim and thinly slice the scallions | Slice the gherkins | Finely chop the capers | Zest the lemon | Put all the prepared vegetables in a large mixing bowl with the lemon zest | Cut the lemon in half and squeeze the juice into the bowl, catching any seeds in your other hand

Separate the herb leaves from any tough stems and finely chop | Add three-quarters of the chopped herbs to the bowl, reserving the rest | Add the egg-free mayo and ¾ teaspoon salt to the bowl and fold everything together

Once the potatoes are cooked, drain them in a colander and run them under cold water until cool enough to handle | Cut into quarters

Add the potatoes to the mixing bowl and fold everything together | Sprinkle with the reserved herbs and serve

CRUNCHY CALI SLAW

Short and sharp, this slaw is quick to make and easy to enjoy. You can really use anything you have left over in your fridge— celery, peppers, radishes, pears, bean sprouts, scallions . . . It's perfect for a BBQ or to serve alongside American-style dishes like our Wild West Wings (see page 160) or Party Poppers (see page 165).

SERVES 6 AS A SIDE

⅓ cup almonds
1 green cabbage (about 12 oz shredded weight)
2 medium red onions
3 carrots
2 Gala or other crisp, sweet apples
½ oz flat-leaf parsley

FOR THE DRESSING
3 limes
generous ¾ cup egg-free mayonnaise
2 tbsp BBQ sauce
1 heaping tbsp mustard
½ tsp hot sauce
2 tsp salt
1 tsp black pepper
a good pinch of cayenne pepper

Preheat oven to 350°F | Sheet pan | Large serving bowl | Grater

Spread the almonds out on the sheet pan | Put the pan in the oven for 8 minutes

Cut the cabbage into quarters, discarding the core, and shred finely | Transfer to a large serving bowl, separating the shreds with your fingers

Peel and thinly slice the onions | Scatter into the bowl, separating the slices, and toss together with your hands

Peel the carrots and grate them using the large holes of a grater (or cut them into fine ribbons) | Add to the bowl and toss to mix

Core, halve, and chop the apples into matchsticks and toss them into the bowl

Pick and roughly chop the parsley leaves | Add most to the bowl, reserving a small handful for garnish

Take the almonds out of the oven, spread them out on a cutting board, and roughly chop into small pieces

Make the dressing | Halve the limes and squeeze the juice into a small bowl | Add the rest of the dressing ingredients and mix with a fork until smooth

Pour the dressing over the slaw and mix everything together | Sprinkle with the reserved parsley and chopped almonds and serve

DOUBLE-COOKED ROSEMARY FRIES WITH QUICK AIOLI

Potatoes are life. We like to double-cook our French fries to make them taste perfect and crispy, pairing them with a simple rosemary salt. Make double or triple batches and freeze them (once chilled) so they're ready whenever you want them.

SERVES 4

4 large russet potatoes (about
    4–5 inches long and 2¼ lb in weight)
2 sprigs fresh rosemary
1 tsp coarse sea salt, plus a little extra
1 tsp black pepper
2 quarts cold water
2 quarts canola oil, for deep-frying

FOR THE QUICK AIOLI
¼ cup egg-free mayonnaise
½ garlic clove
salt

Microplane or fine grater | Pestle and mortar | Large saucepan | Cooling rack set over a sheet pan | Deep-fat fryer, optional | Cooking thermometer

....

Peel the long sides of the potatoes, leaving the ends with the skin on | Cut them into ⅓-inch-thick slices first, then into ⅓-inch sticks

Fill a large bowl (or the sink) with cold water | Rinse the potatoes, submerge them, and leave to soak for 30 minutes

Remove the leaves from the rosemary by running your thumb and forefinger from the top to the base of the stems (the leaves should easily come away) | Finely chop and add to a pestle and mortar with the sea salt and black pepper | Grind to make a rosemary salt

Fill the large saucepan with the water and add a generous pinch of salt | Add the drained potatoes | Turn the heat to medium-high and bring to a boil | Simmer for 5–7 minutes, until barely soft | Carefully transfer to the cooling rack, put the pan in the fridge, and chill for 1 hour | Clean out the pan

Meanwhile, make the aioli | Put the egg-free mayonnaise into a small bowl | Peel the garlic, then use a Microplane or fine grater to grate it into the bowl and mix with a fork | Taste and season to perfection with salt

Pour the oil into the deep-fat fryer or large saucepan, making sure it comes no more than halfway up the sides of the pan, and heat to exactly 320°F | Using a slotted spoon, carefully add two spoonfuls of the fries to the hot oil, making sure they're submerged by at least 1 inch | Fry for 7 minutes, until golden and crispy | Remove with the slotted spoon or fryer basket, gently shaking off any excess oil | Transfer to the cooling rack to drain | Repeat to cook all the fries

Put the fries in a bowl | Sprinkle with the rosemary salt, toss to coat, and serve immediately with the aioli on the side

MASH!

The humble potato, sweet potato, and beet take center stage here, showing us just how creamy and delicious simple ingredients can be. Each of these mash dishes is bursting with subtle, balanced, luxurious flavor, and will add both style and substance to any hearty meal, while the sweet potato and beet mashes will get you well on your way to eating the rainbow.

ROAST SWEET POTATO MASH

SERVES 4 AS A SIDE

3 lb 5 oz sweet potatoes
2 garlic cloves
1 tbsp olive oil, plus extra for drizzling
8 scallions
1 fresh red chili
7 tbsp unsweetened plant-based milk
3½ tbsp dairy-free butter
salt and black pepper

Preheat oven to 390°F | **Line a sheet pan** | **Large saucepan** | **Potato masher**

Peel the sweet potatoes and chop them into 1¼-inch chunks | Spread over the sheet pan and add the garlic cloves | Drizzle with olive oil, sprinkle with salt and pepper, and roast for 30 minutes

Meanwhile, peel and finely dice the scallions | Rip the stem from the chili, remove the seeds, and finely chop | Pour 1 tablespoon oil into the saucepan and add the onion and chili | Fry for 2 minutes, stirring, then take off the heat

Take the pan out of the oven and let cool a little | Squeeze the garlic cloves into a bowl, mash with a potato masher, and add to the pan | Add the sweet potato, milk, and dairy-free butter and mash | Taste, season with salt and pepper, and serve

ROAST BEET MASH

SERVES 4 AS A SIDE

3 raw beets
2¼ lb russet potatoes
2 garlic cloves
6 sprigs fresh thyme
2 tbsp water
2 tbsp olive oil
½ tsp salt, plus a little extra
½ tsp black pepper, plus a little extra
½ tsp chili flakes
4 tbsp dairy-free butter
⅔ cup unsweetened plant-based milk

Preheat oven to 390°F | Loaf pan | Foil | Large saucepan | Blender

Peel and quarter the beets and potatoes | Put the beets into the loaf pan with the garlic and thyme | Pour in the water, drizzle with the oil, and sprinkle with the salt, pepper, and chili flakes | Cover the pan tightly with foil and bake for 45 minutes, or until a sharp knife glides easily into the thickest part of the beet

Meanwhile, put the potatoes in the saucepan | Cover with cold water, add a generous pinch of salt, and put over high heat | Bring to a boil and cook for 15–20 minutes, until tender | Drain and leave to dry, then tip back into the pan | Add the dairy-free butter and milk and mash until smooth

Take the loaf pan out of the oven and leave to cool a little | Squeeze the roasted garlic into the blender, add the beet, and blend | Fold into the mashed potato | Taste, season with salt and pepper, and serve

MUSTARD MASH

SERVES 4 AS A SIDE

2¼ lb russet potatoes
2 large shallots
2 garlic cloves
1 tbsp olive oil
3 tbsp whole-grain mustard
4 tsp dairy-free butter
½ cup unsweetened plant-based milk
salt and black pepper

Large saucepan | Fine grater or Microplane | Skillet | Potato masher

Peel the potatoes and put them in the saucepan | Cover with cold water and sprinkle in a generous pinch of salt | Put over high heat, bring to a boil, and cook for 15–20 minutes, until tender | Drain and leave to dry

Meanwhile, peel and thinly slice the shallots | Peel and grate the garlic

Put the skillet over medium heat and add the oil | Add the shallots and a small pinch of salt | Fry for 3–4 minutes | Add the garlic and stir for 2 minutes

Add the dry potatoes and mash roughly | Add the mustard, dairy-free butter, and milk | Reduce the heat to low and continue to mash until smooth and warmed through | Taste, season with salt and pepper, and serve

Pictured on pages 182–183

ROAST SWEET
POTATO MASH

ROAST BEET MASH

MUSTARD MASH

5

GREENS

Henry's favorite
Mega Mezze Platter

Ian's favorite
Thanksgiving Salad

ORANGE, FENNEL & WATERCRESS SALAD

A really refreshing salad, this works perfectly next to the tagine on page 98 or with any pasta dish. If you have a speed peeler (Y peeler) or a mandoline, use it to create extra-thin slices of fennel. It's also a great dish to make a day ahead or pack into a lunchbox; just keep the dressing in a separate airtight container until you are about to eat.

SERVES 4—6

7 oz sourdough bread
3 tbsp olive oil
3 oranges
2 large fennel bulbs
5 oz blanched almonds
3½ oz watercress
salt and black pepper

FOR THE DRESSING
6 tbsp extra-virgin olive oil
1 tsp whole-grain mustard
1 lemon

Preheat oven to 390°F | Line 2 sheet pans

Tear the bread into large chunks and spread them over one of the pans | Drizzle with the olive oil and sprinkle with a generous pinch each of salt and pepper (you could also sprinkle on some chopped rosemary or thyme for even more flavor) | Place the pan in the oven and cook for 5–10 minutes, turning occasionally, until just golden brown and not too crispy

Peel and segment the oranges, cutting away the pith, and place them in a salad bowl | Cut the fennel in half lengthwise and then slice into very thin strips | Add to the bowl | Reserve any fronds for a garnish

Spread the almonds over the second sheet pan | Put the pan in the oven and bake for 6–8 minutes until golden

To make the dressing, add the olive oil and mustard to a small bowl | Cut the lemon in half and squeeze in the juice, catching any seeds with your other hand | Stir with a fork | Taste and season with salt and pepper

Add the watercress, almonds, and croutons to the salad bowl and toss | Pour on the dressing and toss again to combine | Serve immediately, garnished with a few fennel fronds if you like

THANKSGIVING SALAD

This is one of those rare, hearty salads better suited to cooler times of year. For extra points, use seasonal pumpkins or squashes or try it with broccoli or cauliflower. It's great alongside Christmas dinner leftovers too, with cranberry sauce. You can roast the veg in advance: store it in the fridge and let it reach room temperature before you make the salad.

SERVES 4

3½ oz pecans
7 oz lacinato (Tuscan) kale
2½ cups cooked Puy lentils
2½ oz dried cranberries

FOR THE ROASTED SQUASH
1 small butternut squash (about 1–1½ lb)
2 tbsp olive oil
1 tsp chili flakes
salt and black pepper

FOR THE DRESSING
1 small garlic clove
1 tbsp Dijon mustard
4 tsp maple syrup
2 tbsp apple cider vinegar
6 tbsp extra-virgin olive oil
salt and black pepper

Preheat oven to 390°F | Line 2 sheet pans | Fine grater or Microplane | Jam jar with a lid | Boiling water

....

Start with the roasted squash | Peel the butternut squash, cut it in half, and scoop out the seeds | Cut the halves lengthwise to make 1-inch-wide strips | Lay the strips on a sheet pan, drizzle with the olive oil, and sprinkle with the chili flakes | Lightly season with salt and pepper | Put the pan in the oven and bake the squash for 40 minutes, turning the pieces halfway through

Spread the pecans out on the second sheet pan | Put the pan in the oven and toast for 10 minutes | Remove from the oven and set to one side

Meanwhile, make the dressing | Peel and finely grate the garlic clove | Put the Dijon mustard, maple syrup, apple cider vinegar, olive oil, and grated garlic in the jar, put the lid on, and shake vigorously to combine | Taste and season to perfection with salt and pepper

Trim and discard the tough stems from the kale, then roughly chop | Fill a mixing bowl with boiling water from the kettle | Submerge the kale in the boiling water and blanch for 1 minute, until slightly soft | Drain and set aside

Pour the dressing into a large mixing bowl and tip in the lentils | Stir to evenly coat | Add the dried cranberries and fold them into the lentils

Divide the dressed lentils among bowls | Place the kale and squash on top | Scatter on the toasted pecans and serve immediately

SPICY THAI SALAD

There are so many amazing flavors working together here with oodles of fresh herbs, sweet mango, and a perfectly balanced chili-satay dressing. Double-batch the sauce to serve as a dip for spring rolls or to add a Thai taste to any salad or greens.

SERVES 4

½ cucumber
2 baby bok choy
¼ small red cabbage (about 6 oz)
1 red bell pepper
1 carrot
2 scallions
1 ripe mango
6 tbsp fresh mint leaves
generous ¾ cup cilantro leaves
¼ cup peanuts
2 limes

FOR THE SAUCE
2 limes
2 garlic cloves
1½-inch piece fresh ginger
2 tbsp superfine sugar
2 tbsp sriracha
1 tbsp sesame oil
2 tsp olive oil
¼ cup soy sauce
⅔ cup fresh cilantro leaves
9 tbsp smooth peanut butter
¼ cup water

Peeler | Blender | Pestle and mortar, optional

First prep the vegetables, mango, and herbs for your salad | Halve the cucumber lengthwise and cut it into ribbons using a vegetable peeler | Trim and shred the bok choy and red cabbage | Cut the bell pepper in half, cut out the stem and seeds, and cut into thin strips | Peel the carrot and peel into ribbons | Trim the scallions and cut them lengthwise into thin strips | Slice the mango lengthwise down either side of the pit, spoon out the flesh, and cut into thin strips | Chop the mint and cilantro leaves

Put all the prepped ingredients into a large mixing bowl and gently toss with your hands so they're well mixed

Now make the sauce | Cut the limes in half and squeeze the juice into the blender | Peel and roughly chop the garlic | Peel the ginger by scraping off the skin with a spoon and chop roughly | Add the garlic and ginger to the blender along with the sugar, sriracha, sesame oil, olive oil, soy sauce, cilantro leaves, peanut butter, and water | Blend to a smooth sauce | Pour into a serving pitcher

Crush the peanuts in a mortar or with the end of a rolling pin | Cut the limes into wedges | Divide the salad among bowls, drizzle with a generous helping of the sauce, and sprinkle with the broken peanuts | Serve with 2 lime wedges each

SPINACH & RICOTTA ZUCCHINIOLI

This wonderfully fresh dish was inspired by Matthew Kenney's raw lasagna. Little ravioli-like parcels are filled with a velvety cashew cream. Make double the amount of pesto and save half to serve with pasta; it will keep in an airtight container in the fridge for up to 3 days. To save time, you could use a good-quality store-bought dairy-free pesto instead.

SERVES 4

8 oz cashews
1 red onion
2 garlic cloves
2 zucchini
3½ oz dairy-free cheese
3½ oz fresh spinach
1 oz fresh basil
1 lemon
7 tbsp water
1 tsp salt, plus a little extra
6 tbsp nutritional yeast
2 tbsp olive oil
3½ oz cherry tomatoes
2 oz arugula
black pepper

FOR THE PESTO

2 oz fresh basil
1 garlic clove
1 lemon
3½ oz store-bought toasted pine nuts
⅔ cup extra-virgin olive oil, plus extra for drizzling
¼ tsp salt
1 tbsp nutritional yeast

Medium saucepan of boiling water over high heat | Peeler | Grater | Blender | Skillet

Tip the cashews into the pan of hot water and boil for 20 minutes, until soft

Meanwhile, get your other ingredients ready | Peel and dice the onion and garlic | Trim the zucchini and peel into at least 32 long, thin ribbons | Grate the dairy-free cheese | Roughly chop the spinach | Pick the basil leaves and chop roughly

Drain the cashews and tip them into the blender | Cut the lemon in half and squeeze in the juice, catching any seeds in your other hand | Add the water, 1 teaspoon salt, and the nutritional yeast | Blend to a smooth, thick cream

Put the skillet pan over medium heat | Pour in the olive oil | When the pan is hot, add the onion and cook for 5 minutes until soft | Add the garlic and stir for 2 minutes | Add the cashew cream and dairy-free cheese and stir until melted | Add the chopped spinach and basil and cook for 3 minutes, until wilted | Taste and season | Remove from the heat and leave to cool to room temperature | You should have a really thick mixture

To make your zucchinioli parcels, lay two zucchini ribbons on a clean surface so that they slightly overlap lengthwise | Lay two more ribbons across them, slightly overlapping, to make a large cross shape with two vertical and two horizontal ribbons | Spoon 2–3 tablespoons of the ricotta cream into the center of the cross | Fold the zucchini over the filling to make a neat little parcel | Repeat to make eight zucchinioli

To make the pesto, clean out the blender | Pluck the basil leaves and discard the stems | Peel the garlic | Add both to the blender | Cut the lemon in half and squeeze the juice into the blender, catching any seeds with your other hand | Add the pine nuts, extra-virgin olive oil, salt, and nutritional yeast | Pulse to a pesto consistency

Plate up! | Halve the tomatoes | Divide the arugula and tomatoes among plates | Drizzle with a little extra-virgin olive oil | Flip over the zucchinioli and place them on the plates, drizzling with a touch more oil | Sprinkle with a little salt | Spoon pesto over each portion and serve immediately

MEGA MEZZE PLATTER

The flavors on these sharing plates are second to none. This mezze will wow your guests and they will all be eating and smiling and laughing, and we promise it will be worth the effort! If you're feeling extra adventurous, try adding the Falafel from page 78 and the Tzatziki from page 58. You can even make your own flatbreads using the recipe on page 78—make the thinner versions, which are better for dipping.

SERVES 6

Baba Ganoush (see page 197)
Lemon & Cilantro Hummus (see page 196)
Tabbouleh (see opposite)
Kofta (see opposite)
Batata Harra (see page 196)
6 pita breads or flatbreads
7 oz olives
a handful of small cornichons (or use our Quick Red Onion Pickle, see page 107)

Preheat oven to 350°F | Broiler on high | Line 2 large sheet pans with foil | Food processor | Large skillet | Salad spinner or colander | Clean kitchen towel | Large saucepan

Start by getting the eggplant under the broiler for the **Baba Ganoush**

Next make the **Lemon & Cilantro Hummus**

Then make the **Tabbouleh**

Take the eggplant out of the oven and set aside until you're ready to make the **Baba Ganoush**

Now make the **Kofta** | Once cooked, open the oven door and let the heat lower to 210°F | Put the cooked kofta back in the oven to keep warm

Make the **Batata Harra** and put them in the oven to keep warm

Put the pita breads in the oven to warm through

Finish making your **Baba Ganoush**

Lay out your mezze dishes and serve

Pictured on pages 198–199

KOFTA

MAKES 18

2 zucchini
1 large red onion
3 large garlic cloves
1 oz fresh parsley
1 oz cilantro
2 tbsp olive oil
1 tbsp ground cumin
1 tsp ground coriander
½ tsp chili powder
½ tsp ground cinnamon
2 (14 oz) cans chickpeas
1¾ cups dried breadcrumbs
1 lemon
salt and black pepper

Preheat oven to 350°F | Grater | Clean kitchen towel | Fine grater or Microplane | Skillet | Food processor | Line a large sheet pan

Coarsely grate the zucchini into a bowl | Sprinkle with a pinch of salt and stir to mix | Set aside for 10 minutes | Wrap the grated zucchini in a clean kitchen towel and twist tightly to squeeze out the water

Peel and finely chop the red onion | Peel and finely grate the garlic | Pick the leaves from the parsley and cilantro and discard the stems

Place the skillet over medium heat and add the oil | Add the onion and fry for 7 minutes, until translucent | Add the garlic and stir for 1 minute | Add the cumin, ground coriander, chili powder, and cinnamon and stir them into the onion | Add the grated zucchini, stir for 1–2 minutes, and take the pan off the heat

Pour the contents of the pan into the food processor | Drain and rinse the chickpeas and add to the processor along with the breadcrumbs, chopped parsley, and cilantro | Cut the lemon in half and squeeze in the juice, catching any seeds in your other hand | Blitz to a textured dough | Take the lid off, remove the blade, taste, and season with salt and pepper, stirring them in with a spoon

Split the mixture into 18 pieces (about 2 oz each) and roll between your palms to make long oval shapes | Spread over the sheet pan | Put the pan in the oven and bake for 20 minutes, until cooked through and crisping at the edges | Remove and serve immediately

TABBOULEH

SERVES 6

¾ cup bulgur wheat
¼ cup olive oil
1½ tsp salt
¾ cup boiling water
16 cherry tomatoes
1 medium cucumber
7 oz fresh flat-leaf parsley
15 fresh mint leaves
4 scallions
3 lemons
½ tsp maple syrup
2 tbsp mixed seeds (such as pumpkin, sunflower, sesame, and linseed)

Boiling water

First cook the bulgur wheat | Put the bulgur wheat, 1 tablespoon of the olive oil, and ½ teaspoon of salt into a heatproof mixing bowl | Pour in the boiling water, put a dinner plate on top, and set aside for 30 minutes | Remove the plate, fluff up the bulgur wheat with a fork, and leave to cool to room temperature

Meanwhile, get the rest of the ingredients ready | Quarter the tomatoes | Chop the cucumber into ¼-inch cubes | Rip the leaves from the parsley and finely chop, discarding the stems | Finely chop the mint and scallions | Add the chopped veg and herbs to the bowl | Cut the lemons in half and squeeze in the juice, catching any seeds in your other hand | Add the remaining olive oil and salt, the maple syrup, and seeds | Tip in the bulgur wheat and fold it into the rest of the ingredients before serving

BATATA HARRA (SPICY POTATOES)

SERVES 6

2¼ lb russet potatoes
1 small red onion
3 garlic cloves
¾ oz fresh parsley
¾ oz fresh dill
5 tbsp olive oil
2 tsp chili flakes
2 tsp ground coriander
2 tsp ground turmeric
1 lemon
salt and black pepper

Large saucepan | Fine grater or Microplane | Large skillet

Peel the potatoes and cut them into 1¼–1½-inch chunks | Put them in the saucepan and cover with cold water | Put the pan over high heat, bring to a boil, and cook for 12–15 minutes | Take the pan off the heat and tip the potatoes into a colander | Leave to steam dry for 10 minutes

Meanwhile, peel and finely dice the red onion | Peel and grate the garlic | Pick the leaves from the parsley and discard the stems | Finely chop the dill and parsley

Place the skillet over medium heat and add the oil | Add the onion and stir for 3 minutes, until soft | Add the garlic and stir for 1 minute | Reduce the heat slightly and stir in the chili flakes, ground coriander, and turmeric | Cut the lemon in half and squeeze in the juice, catching any seeds with your other hand | Toss the potatoes in the colander to roughen the edges and add them to the skillet | Turn the heat back up to medium and cook for 15 minutes, gently stirring the potatoes around in the pan occasionally to make sure they're well coated, golden, and have started to crisp up at the edges | Stir in the chopped herbs and salt and pepper to taste | Serve immediately

LEMON & CILANTRO HUMMUS

MAKES ABOUT 1¾ CUPS

1 lemon
1 (14 oz) can chickpeas
1 small garlic clove
2 tbsp tahini
¾ tsp salt, plus more to taste
¼ cup water
2 tbsp olive oil
½ oz cilantro
black pepper, to taste

Food processor

Cut the lemon in half and squeeze the juice into the food processor, catching any seeds with your other hand | Drain and rinse the chickpeas | Peel the garlic

In a food processor, blitz the chickpeas, garlic, tahini, salt, water, and olive oil | Remove the blade

Pick the leaves from the cilantro and discard the stems | Stir the leaves into the hummus

Taste and season to perfection with salt and pepper, transfer to a bowl, and serve immediately

BABA GANOUSH

MAKES ABOUT 2¼ CUPS

3 medium eggplant (about 2 lb)
3 garlic cloves
1 lemon
3 tbsp tahini
⅓ cup + 1 tbsp extra-virgin olive oil
1¼ cups fresh parsley leaves
a few pomegranate seeds, optional
salt

Broiler on high | Line a sheet pan with foil | Salad spinner or colander | Fine grater or Microplane

Place the whole eggplant on the lined sheet pan | Put the pan on the top shelf of the broiler | Broil for 1 hour, turning occasionally, until very, very tender | Remove the pan from the broiler | Pull up the foil around the eggplant and seal the top to make a package | Leave to steam for 10 minutes (or until you're ready to make the baba ganoush)

Open the foil and, when cool enough to handle, slice each eggplant in half lengthwise | Scoop the flesh into a salad spinner or colander | Spin gently to remove all the moisture, or gently press the eggplant in the colander until most of the liquid has dripped out | Transfer to a mixing bowl

Now combine with the rest of the ingredients | Peel and grate the garlic into the bowl | Cut the lemon in half and squeeze in the juice, catching any seeds with your other hand | Stir vigorously for 2 minutes until you have a paste | Stir in the tahini | Slowly add the ⅓ cup olive oil, stirring continuously to allow the mixture to emulsify and become really creamy | Season generously with salt | Taste and add more lemon juice if necessary | Roughly chop the parsley and add most to the bowl, stirring it in

Transfer to a serving dish | Make a small well in the middle and pour in 1 tablespoon olive oil | Garnish with a few more parsley leaves and a handful of pomegranate seeds, if using, and serve

BANG BANG NOODLE SALAD

One of our most epic salads, this dish tastes like Thai takeout but has all the goodness of a salad. Bangin' veg with an incredible Asian dressing, you'll want to make it again and again. Try the dressing with roasted veggies or any Asian- or Thai-flavored meal. Switch out the rice noodles with soba noodles for a higher protein meal or add some pan-grilled tofu.

SERVES 3–4

3½ oz dried rice vermicelli
¼ cup sesame oil
¼ cucumber
1 carrot
1 red bell pepper
1 head bok choy
3 scallions
3 tbsp peanuts
1 fresh red chili
½ oz cilantro
3-inch piece fresh ginger
2 limes
1½ tsp chili flakes
¼ cup peanut butter
2 tbsp soy sauce
3 tsp maple syrup
¼ cup water
1 tbsp vegetable oil
4 portobello mushrooms

Boiling water | Peeler | Saucepan | Food processor | Wok

Prep the vermicelli | Pour the boiling water into a large mixing bowl | Submerge the vermicelli in the hot water and leave them to soak for 5 minutes (or follow the instructions on the package) | Drain the noodles in a sieve and run them under cold water until cool | Tip them back into the bowl | Pour over 1 tablespoon of the sesame oil, toss to coat, and set to one side

Now make the salad | Peel the cucumber into ribbons using a vegetable peeler, discarding the watery middle | Trim and peel the carrot, then peel it into ribbons | Cut the bell pepper in half, cut out the stem and seeds, and slice into long, thin strips | Cut out the thick stem off the bok choy and shred the leaves thinly | Trim the scallions, cut them in half, and then thinly slice them lengthwise | Roughly chop or crush the peanuts | Rip off the stem from the chili and cut it into thin slices | Pick the cilantro leaves and discard the stems

Add the vegetables and herbs you've just prepared to the bowl with the noodles | Toss everything together to combine | Divide among bowls and set to one side

Quickly make the dressing | Peel the ginger by scraping off the skin with a spoon and roughly chop | Zest one of the limes | Cut both limes in half and squeeze the juice into the food processor | Add the lime zest, peeled ginger, 2 tablespoons of the sesame oil, the chili flakes, peanut butter, soy sauce, maple syrup, and water | Blitz to make a sauce

Cut the portobello mushrooms into thin strips | Put the wok over high heat and add the vegetable oil and remaining sesame oil | When the pan is hot, add the mushrooms and fry for 5–6 minutes, until they shrink in size and darken in color

Divide the cooked mushrooms among the bowls | Drizzle with the spicy peanut dressing | Sprinkle with the broken peanuts and sliced red chili and serve immediately

ROMESCO SALAD

We love Barcelona and this dish whisks us away to the wonderful beachfront. We definitely recommend making double the sauce and keeping some for dressing another salad, or for dipping nachos or crudités—and if you like it spicy you could certainly add a little more heat.

SERVES 4

about 10 oz bread (e.g., sourdough)
2 tbsp olive oil
9 oz mixed or cherry tomatoes
1 oz blanched almonds
1 oz hazelnuts
1 (12 oz) jar roasted peppers (or you can make your own by roasting the peppers at 390°F until blackened, then cooling in a bag and peeling)
4 scallions
a small bunch of fresh parsley
2 oz arugula or peppery salad leaves such as lamb's lettuce or mizuna
salt and black pepper

FOR THE DRESSING
½ cup sliced almonds
2 garlic cloves
1 roasted red pepper from the jar for the salad (about 3½ oz)
4½ tbsp tomato paste
½ oz fresh flat-leaf parsley
1 tsp smoked paprika
¼ tsp cayenne pepper
2 tbsp red wine vinegar
⅓ cup extra-virgin olive oil
salt and black pepper

Preheat oven to 350°F | Line 2 sheet pans | Food processor

Remove the crusts from the bread, then cut it into ⅓-inch croutons | Scatter over a sheet pan and drizzle with the olive oil | Sprinkle with generous pinches of salt and pepper | Put the pan in the oven for 12 minutes, turning the croutons halfway through | Remove when golden and crispy

To make the dressing, spread the sliced almonds over the second sheet pan | Put the pan in the oven for 5 minutes, until the almonds are golden brown | Tip into the food processor along with all the dressing ingredients except for the olive oil, salt, and pepper | Blitz until smooth, scraping down the sides of the bowl with a spatula if necessary to combine all the ingredients | While the processor is running, slowly add the olive oil until you have a smooth dressing | Taste and season with salt and pepper | Pour into a serving dish and clean out the food processor

Cut the tomatoes into bite-sized pieces | Tip the blanched almonds and hazelnuts into the clean food processor and pulse to chop roughly | Cut the roasted peppers into 1¼-inch pieces | Trim and thinly slice the scallions

To assemble the salad, add the tomatoes, parsley, roasted peppers, scallions, and salad greens to a large bowl | Sprinkle with the chopped nuts and croutons | Serve in the bowl and toss together at the table just before serving, with the dressing on the side for people to help themselves

CRUNCHY CARNIVAL SALAD

This spicy and sweet salad brings together all our favorite flavors from the Notting Hill Carnival in London—great for a relaxed healthy lunch on a sunny day. Make extra to pack into a lunchbox. It also goes really well with pan-grilled tofu or jackfruit roasted in a spicy jerk or BBQ sauce.

SERVES 6

1 oz cilantro
¼ red cabbage
8 scallions
2 carrots
1 red bell pepper
2 mangoes
1 avocado
1 large fresh red chili
generous 3 tbsp egg-free mayonnaise
1 tsp–1 tbsp West Indian
   hot sauce (Encona)
1 tsp maple syrup
2 limes
1⅓ cups corn kernels
salt and black pepper

FOR THE SWEET POTATOES

2 large sweet potatoes (about 1½ lb)
1 tbsp olive oil
½ tbsp chili flakes
salt and black pepper

FOR THE RICE & BEANS

5 sprigs fresh thyme
2 garlic cloves
1 (14 oz) can kidney beans
1 (13.5 oz) can full-fat coconut milk
7 tbsp water
¼ tsp ground allspice
1 tsp salt
¼ tsp black pepper
1 cup long-grain rice

Preheat oven to 350°F | Sheet pan | String | Medium saucepan

First cook the sweet potatoes | Peel the sweet potatoes and cut them into ¾-inch chunks | Spread over the sheet pan | Sprinkle with the oil, chili flakes, and a little seasoning | Roast for 25–30 minutes, turning halfway

Meanwhile, make the rice and beans | Pick and roughly chop the cilantro leaves and set aside | Tie the cilantro stems and thyme together with string to make a bouquet garni | Peel the garlic | Drain the kidney beans

Put the saucepan over medium heat | Add the coconut milk, water, allspice, salt, pepper, garlic, and bouquet garni and bring to a simmer | Wash the rice under cold water until it runs clear and tip into the saucepan | Stir, reduce the heat to a very gentle simmer, put the lid on, and cook until all the liquid has been absorbed, about 13–16 minutes | Take the pan off the heat | Remove the garlic and bouquet garni | Fold in the kidney beans | Put the lid back on for 5 minutes

Prep the rest of the fresh ingredients | Shred the cabbage | Cut the scallions in half and shred them lengthwise | Peel the carrots and then peel them into ribbons | Trim the bell pepper and slice into thin strips | Slice the mangoes lengthwise down either side of the pit, spoon out the flesh, and slice thinly | Halve and carefully pit the avocado by tapping the pit firmly with the heel of a knife so that it lodges in the pit, then twist and remove | Scoop out the flesh, then slice thinly | Rip the stem from the chili, cut it in half, scrape out the seeds, and slice thinly

Put the egg-free mayonnaise, hot sauce, and maple syrup into a large bowl | Halve one of the limes, squeeze in the juice, and stir to mix | Add the cabbage, scallions, carrots, pepper, chili, cilantro leaves, and corn | Toss to coat in the dressing

Serve the rice into large bowls | Spoon over the roasted sweet potatoes | Pile on the salad and top with the avocado and mango slices | Squeeze more lime over the avocado | Quarter the remaining lime and place a wedge on each bowl | Serve immediately

HEALTHY MEAL PREP

A whole-food, plant-based diet is a really healthy way to live your life and with a little bit of planning it's easy to fit it into your lifestyle. We love to prep healthy meals so that we can grab a meal and go. We prefer to do this a couple of days in advance (rather than making seven days' worth of meals in one go) so that the food tastes deliciously fresh when you eat it. See page 24 for more on meal planning and meal prep.

On the following pages are three easy and tasty recipes that will give you enough meals for two full days. This meal plan is nutritionally balanced with lots of green veg and plenty of color to make sure you get loads of plant-filled energy in your diet—we suggest adding a banana for a snack each day too. And we've broken them down so that you know exactly what to prep and when. See how the meal plan looks on pages 210–211.

GREEN BREAKFAST SMOOTHIES

This smoothie is a fantastic way to fill your body with healthy veg and green is king here. If you pack your diet with greens first thing in the morning it helps you get a head start on a healthy day. Each smoothie is about 3 cups, which is a lot! You can drink half in the morning and take the rest with you in a bottle for an afternoon snack.

MAKES BREAKFAST AND A SNACK FOR 2 DAYS

2 bananas
2 apples
4 oz frozen mixed berries
2 oz mixed nuts
2 tbsp ground flaxseed
5 oz kale
3½ oz spinach
1¼ cups B12-fortified unsweetened plant-based milk
1¼ cups water
¼ cup plant-based protein powder, optional

The night before | 2 freezerproof containers or bags

Peel and roughly chop the bananas | Roughly chop the apples | Divide between the freezerproof containers along with all the berries, nuts, and seeds | Place in the freezer and leave overnight

In the morning | Blender

Place half the kale and half the spinach into the blender with half the milk, half the water, and half the protein powder, if using | Blitz until completely smooth | Take one of the containers out of the freezer and add the contents to the blender | Blend until smooth, then drink the whole thing for breakfast or transfer to a portable container to drink throughout the day (give it a little shake before drinking as it may have separated)

PIRI PIRI PROTEIN LUNCHBOX

This lunchbox is tasty, healthy, and packed full of protein. The tofu is flavored with delicious hot sauce and the rice and peas complement it perfectly, while everything is brought together by a wholesome turmeric hummus. You could use store-bought hummus and hot sauce for speed. However, our Homemade Sambal Chili Sauce and Turmeric Hummus (see page 208) are simply incredible and worth the extra time on prep day.

MAKES LUNCH FOR 2 DAYS

2 (10 oz) blocks tofu
1½ cups canned kidney or other beans
1 (9 oz) package cooked brown rice
¾ oz cilantro
2 oz fresh spinach
1 tsp olive oil
2 tsp hot sauce (store-bought or use
    our Homemade Sambal Chili Sauce,
    see page 208)
3 oz broccolini
½ lemon
½ lime
salt and black pepper

FOR THE QUICK TURMERIC HUMMUS
(or use our Homemade Turmeric
    Hummus, see page 208)
8 oz store-bought hummus
1 tsp ground turmeric
½ tsp cayenne pepper

FOR THE QUICK SPICY MARINADE
(or use our Homemade Sambal Chili
    Sauce, see page 208)
5 tbsp good-quality low-sugar
    hot sauce (we use Cholula)
1 tsp olive oil

The night before | Tofu press or 2 clean kitchen towels and a weight such as a heavy book | Grill pan

Press the tofu using a tofu press or place it between two clean kitchen towels, lay it on a plate, and put a weight on top | Leave for 30 minutes to drain and firm up

Make the spicy marinade by pouring the hot sauce and olive oil into a bowl and mixing with a fork (or follow the recipe on page 208) | Slice the tofu into ⅓-inch-thick slices and add them to the marinade | Leave for 10 minutes

Make the turmeric hummus by putting the hummus, turmeric, and cayenne into a bowl and mixing until completely combined (or follow the recipe on page 208)

Drain the kidney beans and put them into a bowl with the rice | Roughly chop the cilantro and spinach and add them to the bowl | Add the olive oil and hot sauce | Stir everything together | Taste and season to perfection

Put the grill pan over high heat | When it's really hot, add the tofu slices and leave to cook for 3–4 minutes without moving them so they develop distinct, solid char lines | Turn and repeat on the other side | Remove the tofu but leave the pan on the heat

Add the broccolini to the pan and leave to cook for about 4 minutes, until they have char lines underneath | Turn and repeat on the other side | When the broccolini is softened with nice char lines all over, transfer to a plate | Squeeze over the juice of the half lemon, catching any seeds in your other hand

Divide the rice and beans, grilled tofu, broccolini, and hummus between the two containers | Quarter the half lime and put 2 pieces in each box | Refrigerate

In the morning | Don't forget to take your lunchbox with you to work!

Squeeze the lime over your delicious, healthy lunch and enjoy!

HOMEMADE SAMBAL CHILI SAUCE

MAKES ¾ CUP

Blender | Wok or skillet

1–2 garlic cloves
2–3 large shallots (about 3½ oz)
2 fresh chilies
¾-inch piece fresh ginger
1 lemon
1–2 roasted red peppers from a jar
    (about 3½ oz)
½ tsp ground turmeric
1 tbsp oil
¼ cup white wine vinegar
salt and black pepper

Peel the garlic and shallots | Rip the stems from the chilies | Peel the ginger by scraping off the skin with a spoon | Zest half the lemon into the blender | Add all the ingredients except the vinegar, oil, and lemon to the blender and blend to a paste

Place the wok or skillet over medium-high heat and add the oil | When it's hot, add the paste, reduce to a low heat, and cook for about 15 minutes, stirring regularly so it doesn't stick | Add the white wine vinegar | Cut the lemon in half and squeeze in the juice, catching any seeds in your other hand | Stir everything together and remove from the heat | Taste and season to perfection

HOMEMADE TURMERIC HUMMUS

**MAKES 1¼ CUPS,
OR 2 PORTIONS**

Food processor

1 (14 oz) can chickpeas
2 small garlic cloves
1 lemon
1 tsp ground turmeric
1 tsp ground ginger
¾ tsp salt
½ tsp cayenne pepper
¼ cup water
2 tbsp tahini
2 tbsp olive oil

Drain the chickpeas and save the water (aquafaba) for another recipe | Peel the garlic | Cut the lemon in half and squeeze the juice into the food processor, catching the seeds with your other hand | Put all the remaining ingredients into the food processor | Blitz to a smooth paste

EASY TOMATO PASTA WITH PAN-GRILLED ASPARAGUS

This cheeky little pasta dish is so quick to rustle up in the
evening. We use whole wheat pasta as it is higher in fiber.
It's a great recipe for batch cooking—make multiple helpings
of the sauce and store it in the freezer for up to a month.

MAKES DINNER FOR 2 DAYS

PREP
1 oz fresh parsley
1 medium onion
2 garlic cloves
1 red bell pepper (about 3½ oz)
1 medium carrot
1 tbsp olive oil
1 (14.5 oz) can diced tomatoes
1⅔ cups water
1–2 tsp hot sauce
¼ tsp dried oregano
½ tsp chili flakes
1 tbsp nutritional yeast, optional
salt and black pepper

FOR EACH SERVING
3–4 oz dried whole wheat pasta
2 oz asparagus
1 tsp olive oil
½ lemon
1 oz mixed salad greens, to serve
salt

The night before | Fine grater or Microplane | Food processor | Medium saucepan | 2 airtight containers

....

Remove the leaves from the parsley and place them in the fridge either in an airtight container or on top of some paper towels

Peel the onion | Peel and grate the garlic | Cut the bell pepper in half and cut out the stem and seeds | Trim the carrot | Put the parsley stems, onion, carrot, and pepper into the food processor and blitz until finely chopped

Put the saucepan over medium heat and pour in the oil | Tip the chopped vegetables from the food processor into the pan and sauté for 8 minutes, stirring | Add the garlic and sauté for 2 minutes | Add the diced tomatoes, water, 1 teaspoon hot sauce, the oregano, and the chili flakes | Taste and season to perfection, adding more hot sauce if you like | Simmer for 10 minutes, until the sauce is thick | Add the nutritional yeast, if using | Divide between the containers, leave to cool, and then refrigerate

The next day | Large saucepan of boiling salted water over high heat | Grill pan over high heat | Small saucepan, optional

....

Add the pasta to the pan of boiling salted water | Cook following the instructions on the package, drain, and tip back into the pan

Meanwhile, rub the asparagus spears with the oil and lay the spears across the lines of the hot grill pan | Cook for about 5 minutes without moving the spears, until they have black char lines | Turn them over and repeat | Cut the lemon in half | Finish the asparagus with a sprinkling of salt and squeeze over the juice of half the lemon, catching any seeds in your other hand

Take one of the sauce containers from the fridge and reheat the pasta sauce on the stovetop or in the microwave, until piping hot | Take out half the parsley leaves and roughly chop

Add the sauce to the pasta and mix until the pasta is evenly coated | Squeeze over some lemon juice, catching any seeds | Stir in the chopped parsley leaves and mix everything together

Serve the pasta on plates with salad greens and the grilled asparagus

Repeat the following day

DESSERTS

Henry's favorite
Bakewell Tart

Ian's favorite
Empire Biscuits

BANANA BREAD DOUGHNUTS

These doughnuts are a fun, delightfully delicious treat and look beautiful! Get creative with the toppings—the world is your oyster. You could even play about with different icing flavors as well.

MAKES 6 DOUGHNUTS

2 small ripe bananas
   (7 oz peeled weight)
1 cup all-purpose flour
½ tsp baking soda
¼ tsp salt
½ tsp ground cinnamon
¼ cup coconut oil
3 tbsp + 1 tsp coconut sugar
2½ tbsp superfine sugar
2 tbsp unsweetened plant-based milk
½ tsp apple cider vinegar
½ tsp vanilla extract
3 tbsp golden raisins

FOR THE TOPPINGS
¾ cup powdered sugar
1½ tbsp warm water
a pinch of ground cinnamon
¼ tsp vanilla extract
1 oz pecans
½ oz dark chocolate

Preheat oven to 340°F | Food processor | Grease a doughnut pan | Cooling rack

Peel the bananas and put them in the food processor | Add the flour, baking soda, salt, ground cinnamon, coconut oil, coconut sugar, superfine sugar, milk, apple cider vinegar, and vanilla extract and blitz to a smooth cream | Take off the lid and remove the blade | Pour in the raisins and mix them into the batter with a spoon

Carefully spoon the mixture into the doughnut pan, making sure the holes are filled to the top | Put the pan in the hot oven and bake for 25 minutes until a skewer inserted into the middle comes out clean | Remove and transfer the doughnuts to a cooling rack | Leave to cool to room temperature

While the doughnuts are baking, make the toppings | Sift the powdered sugar into a mixing bowl | Add the warm water, ground cinnamon, and vanilla extract and stir everything together to make a thick, smooth icing

Finely chop the pecans | Grate the dark chocolate

Artfully drizzle the icing all over the doughnuts and quickly sprinkle with the pecans and chocolate | Serve immediately

ICE CREAM

We heart ice cream and you can now find bangin' dairy-free versions in stores. But there's something magical about making your own. It's easiest with an ice-cream maker (ours costs $25). However, you can also just use a freezer and a whisk; take it out and stir it occasionally for a smooth texture. Use the basic vanilla recipe and add your own delicious flavorings! The vodka ensures you get a nice soft scoop but you can leave it out if you prefer.

CLASSIC CHOCOLATE

MAKES ABOUT 2 QUARTS

1 lb cashews
3½ oz dark chocolate
2 cups unsweetened plant-based milk
¾ cup amber maple syrup
6 tbsp cocoa powder
¾ tsp xanthan gum
1 tsp chocolate vodka
   (or just use normal vodka)

Large saucepan of boiling water over high heat, optional | Boiling water | Small saucepan | Heatproof bowl | Blender | Ice-cream maker or baking dish and whisk | 2-quart freezer container

....

Put the cashews in the pan of hot water and boil for 15 minutes until they are soft and have rehydrated (or soak them overnight in cold water)

Melt the chocolate | Pour hot water into the small saucepan until it's about 1¼ inches deep and bring to a boil | Reduce the heat to a simmer | Put a heatproof bowl on top of the pan, ensuring the water doesn't touch the bottom | Break half the dark chocolate into the bowl and leave it to melt | Remove and leave to cool a little | Alternatively, melt the chocolate in the microwave in 15-second bursts

Blend all the ice-cream ingredients except for the reserved chocolate in the blender until smooth | Taste and adjust with more maple syrup, cocoa, and/or vodka until you're happy with the flavor

Pour into the ice-cream maker and follow the manufacturer's instructions to make delicious ice cream | Alternatively, pour into the baking dish and put in the freezer until firm, but still pourable, removing occasionally to whisk, if you like, to improve the texture

Melt the reserved chocolate using the method above and drizzle some of it over the bottom of the freezer container | Pour in a layer of ice cream and drizzle with more melted chocolate | Repeat until all the ice cream is used up, finishing with a final drizzle of chocolate | Cover and freeze | When the ice cream has expanded and frozen through, it's ready to serve

BANOFFEE WITH CARAMEL SAUCE

MAKES ABOUT 2 QUARTS

1 lb cashews
3 bananas (about 13 oz peeled weight)
2 cups unsweetened plant-based milk
¾ cup maple syrup
1 tsp vanilla extract
¾ tsp xanthan gum
1 tsp vodka

FOR THE CARAMEL SAUCE
generous ¾ cup full-fat coconut milk
¼ cup light brown sugar
¼ cup golden superfine sugar
¼ tsp sea salt
1 tsp vanilla extract

Large saucepan of boiling water over high heat, optional | Blender | Ice-cream maker or baking dish and whisk | Medium heavy-bottomed saucepan | 2-quart freezer container

....

Put the cashews in the pan of hot water and boil for 15 minutes until they are soft and have rehydrated (or soak them overnight in cold water)

Peel the bananas, then blend all the ice-cream ingredients in the blender until smooth | Taste and adjust the maple syrup, vanilla, and/or vodka until you're happy with the flavor

Pour into the ice-cream maker and follow the manufacturer's instructions to make delicious ice cream | Alternatively, pour into the baking dish and put in the freezer until firm but pourable, removing occasionally to whisk, if you like, to improve the texture

Meanwhile, make the caramel sauce | Place the coconut milk, sugars, and salt in the medium saucepan and put over medium-high heat | Bring to a boil, whisking constantly, and cook for 5–10 minutes, until caramelized and thickened (it will boil up in the pan, so be careful) | Remove from the heat and stir in the vanilla extract | Set aside to cool

Once the ice cream is firm, drizzle some of the caramel into the bottom of the freezer container | Cover with a layer of the just-churned ice cream | Drizzle with more caramel sauce | Repeat to use up all the ingredients | Cover and freeze

Pictured on pages 220–221

CLEAN SLATE VANILLA

MAKES ABOUT 2 QUARTS

1 lb cashews
2 cups unsweetened plant-based milk
¾ cup light agave or maple syrup
2 tbsp vanilla paste
¾ tsp xanthan gum
1 tsp vodka

Large saucepan of boiling water on a high heat, optional | Blender | Ice-cream maker or baking dish and whisk | 2-quart freezer-proof container

....

Put the cashews in the pan of hot water and boil for 15 minutes until they are soft and have rehydrated (or soak them overnight in cold water)

Blend all the ice-cream ingredients in the blender until smooth | Taste and add more vanilla, syrup, and/or vodka if necessary to get the flavor right

Pour into the ice-cream maker and follow the manufacturer's instructions to make delicious ice cream | Alternatively, pour into the baking dish and put in the freezer until frozen, removing occasionally to whisk, if you like, to improve the texture

RASPBERRY RIPPLE COOKIE CRUMBLE

MAKES ABOUT 2 QUARTS

1 lb cashews
2 cups unsweetened plant-based milk
¾ cup light agave or maple syrup
2 tbsp vanilla paste
¾ tsp xanthan gum
1 tsp vodka
5½ oz plant-based chocolate
   sandwich cookies

FOR THE RASPBERRY SAUCE
14 oz raspberries
½ cup golden superfine sugar

Large saucepan of boiling water over high heat, optional | Blender | Ice-cream maker or baking dish and whisk | Medium saucepan | 2-quart freezer container

....

Put the cashews in the pan of hot water and boil for 15 minutes until they are soft and have rehydrated (or soak them overnight in cold water)

Blend all the ice-cream ingredients in the blender until smooth | Taste and add more syrup, vanilla, and/or vodka until you're happy with the flavor

Pour into the ice-cream maker and follow the manufacturer's instructions to make delicious ice cream | Alternatively, pour into the baking dish and put in the freezer until firm, but still pourable, removing occasionally to whisk, if you like, to improve the texture

Meanwhile, make the raspberry sauce | Place the raspberries and sugar in the medium saucepan and put over medium-high heat | Cook, stirring regularly, for 10–15 minutes, until very thick | Remove from the heat and push through a sieve to remove the seeds | Set aside and allow to cool

Once the ice cream is firm, drizzle some of the raspberry sauce into the freezer container | Crumble the cookies and sprinkle a few of the crumbs over the sauce | Cover with a layer of the just-churned ice cream | Drizzle over more raspberry sauce and sprinkle with more cookie crumbs, then gently stir to distribute through the ice cream | Repeat to use up all the ingredients | When the ice cream has expanded and frozen through, it's ready to serve

Pictured on pages 220–221

CLEAN SLATE
VANILLA

BANOFFEE WITH
CARAMEL SAUCE

CLASSIC
CHOCOLATE

RASPBERRY RIPPLE
COOKIE CRUMBLE

NEW YORK–STYLE BAKED STRAWBERRY CHEESECAKE

This cheesecake will whisk you away to a decadent holiday in New York! The idea of using tofu may seem a little strange, but trust us, you are going to love this all-plants cheesecake. Try experimenting with different fruit on top too—bananas, raspberries, or blueberries would all taste incredible. It will keep in the fridge for 3 to 4 days.

SERVES 10—12

14 oz cashews
4 oz graham crackers
4 oz ginger snaps
7 tbsp light olive oil
a pinch of salt
10½ oz dairy-free white chocolate
2 lemons
12 oz silken tofu
2½ cups powdered sugar
2 tbsp coconut oil
3 tsp vanilla extract
14 oz strawberries
¼ cup golden superfine sugar

Preheat oven to 350°F | Baking sheet on the middle rack of the oven | Large pan of boiling water over high heat, optional | Food processor | Line 9-inch springform pan with round of parchment paper (don't grease the sides) | Small saucepan | Heatproof bowl | Blender | Pastry brush | Medium saucepan

....

Put the cashews in the pan of hot water and boil for 15 minutes until soft and rehydrated (alternatively, soak them overnight in cold water) | Drain

Put all the cookies in the food processor and blitz to crumbs | Add the oil and a pinch of salt and pulse to mix | Tip into the lined springform and press firmly until well compacted and even | Put in the oven and bake for 15–20 minutes, until firm | Remove and leave to cool for 10 minutes | Lower the oven temperature to 230°F and put the pan back in

Meanwhile, melt the chocolate | Pour 1¼ inches hot water into the small saucepan and bring to a boil | Lower to a simmer | Put the heatproof bowl on top of the pan, ensuring the water doesn't touch the bottom | Break the chocolate into the bowl and leave to melt (alternatively, melt in the microwave in 15-second bursts) | Remove and leave to cool a little | Separate 2 tablespoons of the chocolate from the main batch

Zest the lemons into the blender, then cut them in half and squeeze in the juice | Add the main batch of chocolate, the silken tofu, drained cashews, powdered sugar, coconut oil, and vanilla extract and blend until smooth

Layer up your cheesecake | Lightly brush the cookie crust with the reserved 2 tablespoons of melted chocolate | Pour in the cheesecake mixture and shake gently to level it | Lightly run your finger over the surface to get rid of any bubbles | Put the springform on the hot baking sheet and bake for 80–90 minutes, until set but still slightly wobbly in the middle | Remove from the oven and run a thin spatula or knife around the edge to separate the cake from the sides, then leave it to cool to room temperature | Transfer the cheesecake to a plate | Refrigerate

Hull the strawberries and halve or quarter them | Put them into the medium saucepan with the sugar | Put the pan over medium heat and stir | Macerate for 2–3 minutes so the sugar melts and strawberries soften slightly | Set aside to cool, then pile onto the cheesecake | Serve

BANANA CHOCOLATE SWIRL PIE

This dish combines our love of banoffee and cinnamon swirls. We use the same technique to create the swirls in our pancakes on page 273 here, to create a beautifully intricate, concentric circle–covered pie crust, encasing a wonderfully sweet banana and cinnamon filling.

SERVES 10

2 (14 oz) cans full-fat coconut milk

1¾ cups + 2 tbsp golden superfine sugar

3 tbsp dairy-free butter, plus extra
    for greasing

2 (11 oz) sheets ready-rolled plant-based
    pie dough

2 tbsp cocoa powder

3½ oz pecans

3–4 large bananas

3 tbsp cornstarch

½ tsp ground cinnamon

a pinch of salt

½ tsp vanilla extract

1 tbsp maple syrup

2 tbsp unsweetened plant-based milk

Banoffee Ice Cream (see page 217),
    for serving

Large saucepan | Small pan, optional | Pastry brush | Grease a 9-inch pie plate | Parchment paper | Pie weights | Sheet pan | Rolling pin or clean, dry wine bottle

....

First make a caramel | Pour the coconut milk and the 1¾ cups superfine sugar into the large saucepan | Put the pan over high heat and bring to a boil, then reduce to a simmer | Cook for 45–50 minutes, stirring frequently, until the liquid has reduced by half and has thickened to a caramel-like consistency | Set aside

Preheat the oven to 390°F | Put the dairy-free butter into a small dish and melt it in the microwave | Alternatively, melt it in a small pan over very low heat | Unroll one sheet of the pastry and lightly brush it with 1 tablespoon of the melted butter | Sift half the cocoa powder over the dough along with 1 tablespoon of the sugar | Roll up the pastry tightly, starting with the longest edge, and put the roll in the fridge for 20 minutes to chill | Repeat with the second sheet of pastry

Take one of the pastry rolls out of the fridge and cut it into ⅓-inch-thick slices | Arrange the slices over the bottom and up the sides of the greased pie plate | Use your fingers to push, press, and manipulate the slices into the dish so that they come together to form one connected, decorative layer of pastry (you might need to use a few slices from the second roll to completely cover the dish)

Brush the pastry with a very thin layer of melted dairy-free butter | Lay a sheet of parchment paper over the pastry and pour the pie weights into it, smoothing them out evenly so that they completely cover the bottom | Place the dish in the oven and bake for 15 minutes | Take out of the oven and remove the parchment paper and pie weight | Continue to bake for 10 minutes | Take the dish out of the oven and put it to one side to cool

Spread the pecans out on the sheet pan | Put the pan in the oven and bake for 5 minutes | Remove and spread the pecans out on a cutting board | Roughly chop

Peel and slice the bananas and put them in a large mixing bowl
| Add the cornstarch, cinnamon, salt, vanilla, and chopped pecans and toss until the bananas are well coated | Pour the coconut milk caramel into the bowl and fold everything together so that it is well mixed | Pour the banana mixture into the pie and smooth it out with the back of a wooden spoon

Lay a large square of parchment paper on a clean surface | Take the second pastry roll out of the fridge and cut it into $1/3$-inch-thick slices | Arrange the slices on the parchment paper to form a tight, solid round (not a ring) | Lay another large sheet of parchment over the top | Use the rolling pin to roll the pastry into a $1/8$-inch-thick sheet of solid pastry

Peel off the top layer of parchment paper | Roll the pastry onto the rolling pin and lift it over the pie | Lay the pastry over the open pie and remove the remaining sheet of parchment | Press the edges of the pastry together to seal the filling inside the pie | Trim any excess pastry from around the dish with a sharp knife or scissors | Crimp the edges with a fork

Make a glaze | Pour the maple syrup and plant-based milk into a small dish and mix with a fork | Brush the top of the pie with the glaze and put it in the oven for 30–35 minutes, until golden and crisp

Take the pie out of the oven and allow it to cool to room temperature before cutting into slices | Serve with scoops of Banoffee Ice Cream

Pictured on pages 226–227

EMPIRE BISCUITS

We discovered Empire biscuits on a trip to Glasgow and were wowed by their jammy deliciousness. If you're feeling fancy, use cookie cutters to make fun shapes, and experiment with different jam fillings. We've also included a recipe for a simple shortbread. The cookies and shortbread will keep for a week or so in an airtight container.

MAKES 10

8½ oz dairy-free butter, at room temperature

½ cup + 2 tbsp superfine sugar

2¾ cups all-purpose flour, plus extra for dusting

1½ tsp vanilla extract

6 tbsp raspberry jam

2 cups powdered sugar

3 tbsp warm water

Preheat oven to 390°F | **Line 2 baking sheets with parchment paper** | **Clean work surface dusted liberally with flour** | **Rolling pin or clean, dry wine bottle** | **2½-inch round biscuit cutter** | **Cooling rack**

Put the dairy-free butter and superfine sugar into a mixing bowl and beat together with a wooden spoon | Sift the flour into the bowl | Add 1 teaspoon of the vanilla extract and fold everything together until you have a nice soft dough

Tip the dough onto the floured work surface and roll it out to ¼ inch thick | Cut out as many cookies as you can | Collect the scraps and re-roll them to use up all the dough | Arrange on the lined baking sheets | Put the sheets in the oven and bake for 12–15 minutes, until the cookies are turning golden in color | Take the sheets out of the oven | Transfer the cookies to a cooling rack and leave to cool to room temperature

Carefully spread ½ teaspoon raspberry jam onto half the cookies | Sandwich with the remaining cookies, pressing down gently to glue them together

Make the icing | Put the powdered sugar, remaining vanilla extract, and warm water into a small bowl and mix until you have a thick icing | Spread an equal amount of icing over each cookie | Refrigerate for 10 minutes to firm up and serve

SUPER-SIMPLE SHORTBREAD

If you would prefer to make shortbread fingers, follow the recipe for Empire Biscuits to make the dough | Roll it out to ⅓ inch thick, then cut into fingers 2¾ inches long and 1 inch wide | Gather any scraps and re-roll to make more fingers | Transfer to a lined baking sheet | Gently prick each finger with a fork for decoration and sprinkle with a little superfine sugar

Put the baking sheet in the oven for 15–20 minutes, until the shortbread fingers are light golden brown | Remove from the oven and transfer to a cooling rack | Leave to cool before serving

BANANA BREAD BLONDIES

These blondies are freakishly good! Arranging the bananas on top makes them look totally awesome. To speed up the process, use a food processor or stand mixer. The blondies will keep for up to 4 days in an airtight container.

MAKES 12

4½ oz almonds
4 bananas—2 ripe (9 oz peeled weight) and 2 firm
9 tbsp peanut butter
6 tbsp maple syrup
¼ cup vegetable oil
6 tbsp unsweetened plant-based milk
1 tbsp vanilla extract
scant 2 cups all-purpose flour
6 tbsp + 2 tsp superfine sugar
1 tsp baking powder
½ tsp baking soda
¼ tsp sea salt
4½ oz dark chocolate
1 tbsp light brown sugar

Preheat oven to 350°F | Sheet pan | Pestle and mortar, food processor, or the end of a rolling pin | Line an 8 x 12-inch baking pan with parchment paper | Small pan and heatproof bowl, optional

Spread the almonds out over the sheet pan, put the pan in the oven, and bake the almonds for 8–10 minutes, until deeply golden | Remove and set aside to cool

Put the ripe bananas in a mixing bowl and mash them with a fork | Add 6 tbsp of the peanut butter, the maple syrup, vegetable oil, milk, and vanilla extract and stir until well combined

Combine the dry ingredients | Pour the flour, superfine sugar, baking powder, baking soda, and sea salt into a separate mixing bowl and combine with a fork | Tip the dry ingredients into the wet ingredients and fold everything together to combine and form a smooth batter

Break the roasted almonds into small chunks using a pestle and mortar, food processor, or the end of a rolling pin | Cut the chocolate into ¼-inch pieces | Add 3½ oz of the broken almonds and 3½ oz of the chocolate chunks to the bowl and fold them into the batter | Transfer to the baking pan and smooth the top with a spatula or the back of a spoon

Dollop the remaining peanut butter over the top of the cake | Sprinkle the remaining almonds over the top and lightly press them into the batter | Peel the firm bananas, cut them in half lengthwise, and gently press the slices into the top of the cake, seed side up | Sprinkle the brown sugar over the bananas | Put the pan in the oven and bake for 35 minutes, until golden brown on top

Melt the remaining chocolate | Pour ¾ inch water into a small pan and bring to a simmer | Place a heatproof bowl over the pan, ensuring the bottom of the bowl doesn't touch the water | Break the remaining chocolate into the bowl and leave to melt (alternatively, melt in the microwave in 15-second bursts) | Drizzle the melted chocolate over the cake | Cut into 12 pieces and serve

BAKEWELL TART

We grew up near the small town of Bakewell, famous for their pudding, so their proud creation is close to our hearts. This version tastes incredible, with almond and cherry flavors in every bite. It actually tastes even better the next day. The rhubarb is optional, but we find a little fruit lightly poached in sugar syrup does a great job of adding color to the plate.

SERVES 8–10

2 cups almond flour
1½ cups all-purpose flour
5 tbsp superfine sugar
1 tbsp demerara sugar
a pinch of salt
¼ cup olive oil, plus extra for greasing
¼ cup unsweetened almond milk
¼ tsp almond extract
powdered sugar, for dusting
sliced almonds, for sprinkling
BOSH! Quick Custard (see opposite)
   or dairy-free ice cream (store-bought
   or see our recipe on page 218), for
   serving, optional
Poached Rhubarb (see opposite),
   for serving, optional

FOR THE COMPOTE
9 oz cherries
9 oz raspberries
6 tbsp golden superfine sugar
½ vanilla bean
1 lemon

FOR THE FRANGIPANE
7 tbsp coconut oil
½ cup golden superfine sugar
2 cups almond flour
2 tbsp cornstarch
²/₃ cup unsweetened almond milk
2 tsp vanilla extract
1 tsp almond extract
a pinch of salt

Preheat oven to 340°F | Medium saucepan | Deep 9-inch tart pan with removable bottom, greased with olive oil | Parchment paper | Pie weights | Small pan, optional | Stand mixer or hand-held beaters | Cooling rack

....

First make the compote | Pit the cherries and put them in the cold saucepan | Add the raspberries and superfine sugar | Cut the vanilla bean in half lengthwise with a sharp knife, scrape out the seeds and add them to the pan | Zest in the lemon, then cut it in half and squeeze in the juice, catching any seeds with your other hand | Put the pan on medium heat and bring to a simmer | Cook for 14–16 minutes, stirring occasionally, until the mixture is thickened and almost jam-like | Take the pan off the heat and set to one side to cool and thicken

To make the tart shell, put the almond flour into a mixing bowl | Stir in the flour, sugars, and salt until well mixed | Pour the olive oil, almond milk, and almond extract into a measuring cup, stir, and then pour the mixture into the bowl | Mix well with a wooden spoon until a dough forms | Put the dough into the center of the greased tart pan and use your hands to carefully and firmly press it out to evenly cover the bottom and up all around the sides of the pan

Lay a piece of parchment paper over the crust and pour the pie weights into it to weigh down the pastry as it cooks | Put the pan in the hot oven and bake for 15 minutes | Take the pan out of the oven, remove the parchment paper and pie weights, and put the tart back in the oven for 6–8 minutes longer, until the pastry is turning golden | Remove from the oven and set aside to cool to room temperature | Reduce the oven temperature to 320°F

To make the frangipane, first soften the coconut oil by warming it for a few seconds in the microwave, if necessary (or in a small pan over medium heat) | Spoon the softened coconut oil and sugar into the bowl of the stand mixer and beat for 2 minutes (or use a mixing bowl and beat with hand-held beaters until you have a custard consistency) | Add the almond flour, cornstarch, almond milk, vanilla extract, almond extract, and salt and beat for another minute

Spread the thickened compote evenly over the base of the cooled tart | Pour the frangipane mixture over the bottom compote and smooth it out with a spatula or the back of a spoon | Put the tart back in the oven and bake for 40–45 minutes, until the top of the tart is turning golden

Remove the tart from the oven and leave it to stand on a cooling rack for 30 minutes to firm up | Carefully remove the tart from the pan | Serve at room temperature in slices, finished with a dusting of powdered sugar and a sprinkling of sliced almonds | Top with BOSH! Quick Custard or dairy-free ice cream and a couple of pieces of Poached Rhubarb, if you like

BOSH! QUICK CUSTARD

MAKES ABOUT 1²/₃ CUPS

Small saucepan over medium heat | Whisk

2 cups + 2 tbsp unsweetened almond milk
1 vanilla bean
½ cup superfine sugar
2 tbsp cornstarch
a very small pinch of ground turmeric

Pour the almond milk into the saucepan and bring to a gentle simmer | Cook for 5 minutes | Cut the vanilla bean in half lengthwise with a sharp knife, scrape out the seeds, and add them to the saucepan along with the sugar | Whisk everything together with a wooden spoon | Spoon a little of the milk mixture into a small bowl and whisk in the cornstarch until completely smooth, then add it back into the pan | Sprinkle in the turmeric and whisk until the custard takes on its color | Serve hot

POACHED RHUBARB

MAKES ABOUT 1 lb

Small saucepan over medium heat

14 oz fresh rhubarb
1¾ cups superfine sugar
1 cup water

Cut the rhubarb into batons | Pour the sugar and water into the pan and bring to a boil | Carefully add the rhubarb batons to the boiling sugar syrup | Take the pan off the heat and leave the rhubarb to poach for no more than 5 minutes | Carefully remove the rhubarb from the pan and transfer to a plate to serve

Pictured on pages 234–235

MINI BANOFFEE MERINGUES

It's a joyous and magical experience to watch a drizzle of chickpea water turn into a fluffy, sweet meringue mix! Ideally, use a stand mixer with a whisk attachment for this recipe as in our experience hand-whisks don't have the power to get the chickpea water to stiff peaks.

MAKES 18

9 tbsp aquafaba (the drained water
   from a 14 oz can chickpeas)
½ tsp cream of tartar
½ cup superfine sugar
2–3 bananas
1 oz dark chocolate

FOR THE CARAMEL SAUCE
¾ cup superfine sugar
½ cup full-fat coconut milk
a pinch of salt
½ tsp dairy-free butter

FOR THE CASHEW CREAM
5 oz cashews
2½ cups full-fat coconut milk
2 tbsp powdered sugar
1 tsp vanilla extract
½ banana

Stand mixer | Line 3 baking sheets with parchment paper | Preheat oven to 350°F | Skillet | Small saucepan | Blender

....

Pour the aquafaba into the mixer | Turn the mixer on to high and leave it running | Add the cream of tartar and continue to beat | After 2 minutes add the superfine sugar, one spoonful at a time | Beat on high for 10–15 minutes | It's ready when the aquafaba has magically transformed into a thick, meringue-like mixture that won't fall off a spoon turned upside down

Spoon the meringue mixture onto the lined baking sheets to make nests about 3 inches wide, no more than ½ inch high, and smooth the top, leaving ¾ inch between them | You should end up with about 18 nests (you can draw 3-inch circles on the parchment paper, then flip over the paper and use them as templates)

Put the baking sheets in the oven and immediately reduce the heat to 210°F | Bake for 2 hours, then turn off the heat, leave the door closed, and let the meringues cool completely, preferably overnight | Cooling the meringues overnight in the oven allows them to set properly and reduces the chances of them cracking due to sudden changes in temperature.

To make the caramel sauce, put the skillet over medium heat | Pour in the sugar, 5 tbsp of the coconut milk, and the salt | Bring to a boil, whisking continuously | Once the mixture has turned caramel in color, about 10–15 minutes, remove from the heat | Add the rest of the coconut milk and the dairy-free butter, stir through, and transfer to a heatproof bowl

To make the cashew cream, put the small saucepan over medium heat | Add the nuts and 1⅔ cups of the coconut milk | Bring to a boil, then reduce the heat and simmer until most of the coconut milk has evaporated | Transfer to the blender | Add the powdered sugar, vanilla, and remaining ¾ cup coconut milk | Add the banana half to the blender | Blend until really smooth

Place your meringue nests on serving plates | Peel 2–3 bananas and cut them into long diagonal slices (the longer they are the more beautiful they will look) | Lay half the slices on top of the meringues | Cover the bananas with dollops of cashew cream | Top with 1 or 2 more banana slices and lashings of caramel sauce | Finely grate the chocolate over them and serve

CHOCOLATE MIRROR CAKE

Mirror, mirror on the wall, who's the tastiest of them all? What can we say? This cake is simply stunning. It's decadent, delicious, and totally luxurious—a real showstopper. Bake it for a birthday; you'll wow the whole party.

SERVES 12

1 cup light brown sugar
1 cup superfine sugar
1¼ cups cocoa powder
3⅓ cups self-rising flour
2 tsp baking powder
¼ tsp salt
4 tsp vanilla extract
2 tsp apple cider vinegar
1 cup light olive oil
1⅔ cups unsweetened plant-based milk
7 tbsp maple syrup

FOR THE CHOCOLATE BUTTERCREAM FILLING
7 oz dark chocolate
2½ cups powdered sugar
generous ¾ cup coconut cream
½ cup + 2 tbsp cocoa powder
a pinch of salt
1 tbsp unsweetened plant-based milk, if needed

FOR THE CHOCOLATE MIRROR GLAZE
5 tsp agar flakes or 1½ tsp agar powder
¾ cup + 2 tbsp water at room temperature
1¾ oz dark chocolate
½ cup coconut cream
3 tbsp maple syrup
a pinch of sea salt
½ cup + 2½ tbsp superfine sugar
½ cup + 2 tbsp cocoa powder
2 tsp cornstarch
1 tbsp vanilla extract
4–6 tbsp unsweetened plant-based milk, optional

Preheat oven to 350°F | Grease and line the bottoms of two 8-inch springform pans with rounds of parchment paper | Cooling rack | Medium saucepan | Heatproof bowl | Stand mixer or hand-held beaters | Spatula | Small saucepan

First make the cake batter | Measure the sugars, cocoa powder, flour, baking powder, and salt into a bowl and mix well | In a separate bowl, combine the vanilla, apple cider vinegar, olive oil, plant-based milk, and maple syrup and mix well | Pour the wet ingredients into the dry ingredients and mix thoroughly

Divide the batter between the prepared pans | Place the pans in the oven and bake for 30 minutes, until a skewer inserted into the center of the cakes comes out clean | Set aside for 5 minutes to cool slightly, then remove from the pans and leave to cool completely on the cooling rack

To make the buttercream filling, pour enough water into the saucepan so that it is a quarter full | Place the pan over medium heat and put the heatproof bowl on top, ensuring the bottom of the bowl doesn't touch the water | Bring the water to a boil | Meanwhile, chop the chocolate into pieces | Put the chopped chocolate into the bowl and stir regularly until it is completely melted, then carefully remove the bowl and turn off the heat | Set aside to cool slightly, then pour into the stand mixer or into a mixing bowl | Add the powdered sugar, coconut cream, cocoa powder, and salt | Beat to combine, adding the milk if needed to thin the buttercream to a thick but spreadable consistency

When the cakes are completely cooled, spread one of the layers with half the buttercream and sandwich the cakes together | Spread the remainder of the buttercream evenly all over the cake, using a spatula to make it as even and smooth as possible | Place in the fridge to chill for several hours

To make the mirror glaze, place the agar in a small saucepan and cover it with the ¾ cup water | Leave to bloom for 10 minutes | Finely chop the dark chocolate | Place the pan over medium heat and bring to a boil | Simmer for 5 minutes, until the agar has completely dissolved | Add the coconut cream, maple syrup, salt, and sugar to the pan | Stir and simmer for a few more minutes | Add the cocoa powder, stirring constantly to stop the mixture from catching on the bottom | When the cocoa powder has completely dissolved, add the dark chocolate

Put the cornstarch into a small cup and add the 2 tablespoons water | Stir to make a slurry | Add this to the chocolate sauce and continue to cook until the mixture comes to a boil and has thickened | Remove from the heat and add the vanilla extract | Strain the mixture through a sieve into a large bowl | Check the consistency and stir in 4–6 tablespoons plant-based milk if the icing is too thick to pour | Set aside to cool, stirring frequently, for 5 minutes; it should be warm to the touch but not set | Pour into a small pitcher

Remove the cake from the fridge and place it on a cooling rack set over a sheet pan | Pour the cooled glaze over the cake, rotating the cake to ensure it is evenly covered and working quickly as the glaze will set fast | Pop any bubbles that appear in the glaze with a skewer | Put the cake back in the fridge to set for at least 2 hours or even overnight

Pictured on pages 240–241

LEMON DRIZZLE LOAF CAKE

Lemon drizzle cake is a classic in the UK, and this recipe is probably one of the best we've tasted. It's sugary sweet with the incredible tangy lemon drizzle to give it that perfect balance. Make sure to drizzle the sauce all over the cake and not just the middle, to ensure an even, rounded top.

SERVES 10

1²/₃ cups self-rising flour
¾ cup ground almond flour
1 cup superfine sugar
1 tsp baking powder
a pinch of salt
2–3 lemons
½ cup light olive oil
¾ cup unsweetened plant-based milk

FOR THE DRIZZLE
1 lemon
½ cup demerara sugar

Preheat oven to 350°F | Line a large 3 lb loaf pan with parchment paper and grease it with a little oil | Skewer or toothpick

First make the cake batter | Tip the self-rising flour, almond flour, superfine sugar, baking powder, and salt into a bowl | Mix well with a fork

Zest 2 lemons into a separate bowl, then cut them in half and squeeze the juice until you have 3 tbsp (use the third lemon if necessary), catching any seeds in your other hand | Add the juice to the bowl along with the olive oil and plant-based milk and stir everything together

Pour the wet ingredients into the dry ingredients and fold everything together until well mixed

Spoon the cake batter into the prepared loaf pan | Put the pan in the oven and bake for 30–35 minutes, until a skewer inserted in the middle comes out clean

While the cake is cooking, make the drizzle | Zest the lemon into a mixing bowl | Cut the lemon in half and squeeze in the juice, catching any seeds | Tip the demerara sugar into the bowl and stir it around with a fork until the sugar dissolves

Take the cake out of the oven and poke holes in the top with a skewer or toothpick | Pour the lemon sugar mixture over the top of the loaf cake, ensuring an even coverage all the way to the sides | Leave to cool in the pan, then cut into slices and serve

CLASSIC VICTORIA SPONGE

A British classic, this Victoria sponge is everything you could want. Not only does it look beautiful, it tastes even better. With the fluffy sponge and smooth buttercream, we guarantee this is your new favorite cake. This makes a lot of buttercream. It will get messy if you lather it on thickly but that's all part of the fun!

SERVES 10

4¼ cups all-purpose flour
1¾ cups + 1 tbsp superfine sugar
2 tsp baking powder
2 tsp baking soda
1½ tsp salt
⅔ cup light olive oil
1⅔ cups unsweetened plant-based milk
3 tbsp vanilla extract
2 tsp apple cider vinegar
5 tbsp raspberry jam
2 oz fresh raspberries
powdered sugar, to dust

FOR THE VANILLA BUTTERCREAM FILLING
5 tbsp dairy-free butter
5 tbsp vegetable shortening
2½ cups powdered sugar
2 tsp vanilla paste or extract
a large pinch of salt

Preheat oven to 350°F | Line two 8-inch cake pans with rounds of parchment paper | Cooling rack | Stand mixer or handheld beaters

First make your cake batter | Tip the flour, sugar, baking powder, baking soda, and salt into a bowl and mix well | Pour the oil, milk, vanilla extract, and vinegar into a separate bowl and mix together | Pour the wet ingredients into the dry ingredients and mix well

Divide the batter between the two cake pans | Place the pans in the oven and bake for 30–35 minutes, until a skewer inserted into the center of the cakes comes out clean | Take the pans out of the oven and put them to one side on a cooling rack to cool to room temperature

Now make the buttercream filling | Put the dairy-free butter and vegetable shortening in the mixer or a bowl and beat until smooth | Gradually add the powdered sugar while continuing to beat the butter | Once all the powdered sugar is mixed in, add the vanilla paste and salt and stir | Put the bowl in the fridge to chill

When you're ready to serve the cake, take the buttercream out of the fridge | Use a knife to level the top of one of the cooled cake layers so the other one will sit correctly on it | Place the leveled cake on a serving plate and spread the top with a thick layer of the buttercream | Spoon the jam over the cream | Place the second cake layer on top and sift some powdered sugar over the top | Decorate with raspberries | Cut into slices and serve

KNICKERBOCKER GLORY & BANANA SPLIT

If you're looking to take your dessert game to the next level, try these British classics. You can use our ice-cream recipes from pages 216—218 or, of course, you can cheat and use store-bought. Feel free to pick and choose your toppings too—the candied nuts, chocolate syrup, and raspberry syrup will all keep well for a day or so.

KNICKERBOCKER GLORY

MAKES 4

4 parfait glasses

7 oz fresh strawberries and raspberries
Chocolate Syrup (see page 248)
Raspberry Syrup (see page 249)
Classic Chocolate Ice Cream
  (see page 216)
Raspberry Ripple Cookie Crumble
  Ice Cream (see page 218)
Soft Whipped Cream (see page 249)
4 plant-based chocolate sandwich
  cookies
Candied Peanuts (see page 248)
1 (1 oz) bag plant-based popcorn
4 maraschino cherries
4 dairy-free ice cream fan wafers

Hull the strawberries and cut them in half | Drop some strawberry halves and whole raspberries into the bottom of a glass

Drizzle the sides of the glass with Chocolate and Raspberry Syrups

Now add the ice cream | Drop in a scoop each of the Chocolate and Raspberry Ripple Cookie Crumble Ice Creams

Drizzle with more syrup | Spoon some Soft Whipped Cream on top | Repeat to make all the sundaes

Now you can decorate your sundaes | Break the cookies into pieces | Sprinkle the sundaes with the Candied Peanuts, popcorn, cherries, and broken cookies | Wedge a fan wafer into each one and serve

BANANA SPLIT

MAKES 4

4 serving dishes

7 oz fresh strawberries and raspberries
4 bananas
Banoffee Ice Cream (see page 217)
Chocolate Syrup (see below)
Soft Whipped Cream (see opposite)
Candied Peanuts (see below)
8 maraschino cherries

First get all your ingredients ready | Hull the strawberries and halve them | Peel the bananas, cut them in half lengthwise, and lay them in the serving dishes

To assemble your splits, scoop the Banoffee Ice Cream on top of the bananas | Drizzle with Chocolate Syrup | Top with the Soft Whipped Cream, berries, Candied Peanuts, and cherries | Give them a final drizzle of Chocolate Syrup and serve

CHOCOLATE SYRUP

MAKES A GENEROUS ¾ CUP

Medium saucepan

7 tbsp maple syrup
5 tbsp water
1 tbsp sugar
a pinch of salt
5 tbsp cocoa powder
1 oz dark chocolate
1 tsp vanilla extract

Put the maple syrup, water, sugar, and salt into the saucepan and place it over medium heat | Bring to a boil and cook for 1 minute | Reduce the heat to low, add the cocoa powder, and whisk until completely dissolved | Remove from the heat and stir in the chocolate, broken into pieces, and vanilla extract | Leave to cool before using

CANDIED PEANUTS

MAKES ABOUT 7 oz

Large heavy-bottomed skillet over medium heat | Line a baking sheet with parchment paper

½ cup superfine sugar
2 tbsp water
5 oz unsalted peanuts
a large pinch of coarse sea salt
a pinch of ground cinnamon

Pour the sugar and water into the pan | Cook for a few minutes, stirring frequently, until the liquid seizes and the sugar crystallizes | Lower the heat and quickly stir in the peanuts | Continue to cook until the nuts are golden, stirring constantly and scraping up any syrup collecting in the bottom of the pan to coat the peanuts | Just before they're cooked, sprinkle with the salt and cinnamon and stir them in | Tip the peanuts onto the lined baking sheet and leave to cool completely, then break up any clumps and serve

Pictured on page 246

RASPBERRY SYRUP

MAKES A GENEROUS ¼ CUP

Medium saucepan

14 oz raspberries
½ cup superfine sugar

Put the raspberries and sugar in the saucepan and place over medium heat | Bring to a boil and cook for about 10 minutes, until the ingredients have reduced to a thick syrup | Pass through a sieve into a container and set aside to cool to room temperature

SOFT WHIPPED CREAM

MAKES ABOUT 1⅓ CUPS

Medium saucepan | Blender

5 oz cashews
2 cups full-fat coconut milk
¼ cup powdered sugar
2 tsp vanilla extract or paste

Place the cashews in the saucepan with 1⅔ cups of the coconut milk | Place the pan over medium heat, bring to a boil, and simmer for 15–20 minutes, until most of the coconut milk has evaporated | Transfer to the blender with the rest of the ingredients and blend until smooth | Chill completely before using

YULE LOG

One of Henry's (and his sister, Alice's) favorite dishes from childhood, this is decadent and packed with sweetness—perfect for the festive season! It firms up a little as it cools, so make it a day in advance. Upgrade the decoration by shaving on some chocolate with a Microplane or by melting a thin layer of chocolate onto a baking sheet, letting it harden, and scraping it off. You can also adorn with holly and cranberries.

SERVES 8–10

scant ¾ cup aquafaba (the drained water from 1–2 [14 oz] cans chickpeas)
½ tsp cream of tartar
¾ cup light brown sugar
½ cup + 2 tbsp cocoa powder
¾ cup all-purpose flour
1 tsp baking soda
¼ tsp ground cinnamon
¼ tsp salt
2 tsp vanilla extract
1 tsp cider vinegar
5 tbsp light olive oil
unsweetened plant-based milk, for thinning, optional
powdered sugar, for dusting
cocoa powder, for dusting
1¾ oz dark chocolate, for grating over the top

FOR THE FROSTING
14 oz dark chocolate
2 cups powdered sugar
1⅔ cups coconut cream
1¼ cups cocoa powder
a pinch of salt

Preheat oven to 350°F | Grease a 9 x 13-inch jelly-roll pan or an 8 x 12-inch sheet pan with light olive oil, line with parchment paper, and grease again | Boiling water | Stand mixer or food processor fitted with the whisk or beater attachment | Medium saucepan | Heatproof bowl

Pour the aquafaba into the mixer or food processor and switch it on to high | With the motor running, add the cream of tartar and leave to run for 3 minutes, until the mixture becomes foamy and starts to thicken | Add the brown sugar, a tablespoon at a time, waiting for the sugar to be completely incorporated before adding more | Run for 2–3 more minutes, then switch off the machine and remove the bowl

In a separate bowl, sift together the cocoa powder, flour, baking soda, cinnamon, and salt | Stir together to mix thoroughly | In another bowl combine the vanilla extract, cider vinegar, and oil | Pour the dry ingredients into the aquafaba mix and gently fold together | Once fully combined, add the wet ingredients and mix well | Thin the mixture with a little milk if necessary | Pour the batter into the prepared pan and spread it out evenly with a spatula or the back of a metal spoon

Put the pan in the oven for 20 minutes | Remove and run a knife around the edges of the cake to loosen it | Leave to cool completely, then transfer to a cutting board | Cut lengthwise into 3 rectangles, one slightly narrower than the other, about 3⅛ inch, 3⅛ inch, and 2¾ inch

To make the frosting, pour hot water into the saucepan, about 1¼ inches deep, and bring to a boil | Reduce to a simmer | Put the heatproof bowl on top, ensuring the water doesn't touch the bottom | Break the chocolate into the bowl and leave to melt | Remove and leave to cool a little | Alternatively, melt the chocolate in the microwave | Add the cooled (but not cold) chocolate to the mixer or food processor, pour in the remaining frosting ingredients, and beat to a smooth, thick frosting

Layer the cake slices on top of each other with the narrower one on top | Cut off a quarter of the cake at a 45-degree angle | Separate the slices and place one large slice on a serving board | Lay a large "branch" piece alongside at an angle | Spread with frosting | Lay the other large slices over the top and spread with frosting | Top with the final, smaller pieces | Cover the whole cake with the remaining frosting and use a fork to create bark patterns | Dust with powdered sugar and cocoa powder | Leave to firm up for at least an hour, then grate the chocolate over and serve

NOTELLA CHRISTMAS TREE

The perfect Christmas dessert (or indulgent breakfast?), this looks beautiful and is so much fun to make. Store leftover chocolate hazelnut spread in sterilized jars (see page 39). Or double-batch the spread as it will keep in the fridge for up to a month. Add a pinch of cinnamon, nutmeg, and ground cloves for extra festive flavor.

SERVES 8–10

2 (10 oz) sheets ready-rolled plant-based puff pastry
1½ tbsp dairy-free butter
2 tbsp powdered sugar

FOR THE CHOCOLATE HAZELNUT SPREAD
7 oz blanched hazelnuts
½ tsp salt
7 oz dark chocolate
⅔ cup maple syrup
7 tbsp unsweetened plant-based milk, plus a little more for brushing

Preheat oven to 350°F | Sheet pan | Blender | Boiling water | Saucepan | Heatproof bowl | Pastry brush | Small pan, optional | Baking sheet | Ruler

....

Spread the hazelnuts out on the sheet pan | Put the pan in the oven for 10 minutes | Transfer the pan to a heatproof surface and let it cool to room temperature

Put the cooled hazelnuts and salt in the blender and blend to a smooth, thick nut butter, scraping down the sides occasionally to make sure it's all incorporated

Melt the chocolate | Pour hot water into the saucepan until it's about 1¼ inches deep and bring to a boil | Reduce the heat to a simmer | Put the heatproof bowl on top of the pan, ensuring the water doesn't touch the bottom | Break the dark chocolate into the bowl and leave it to melt | Remove and leave to cool a little | Alternatively, melt the chocolate in the microwave in 15-second bursts

Pour the melted chocolate, maple syrup, and milk into the blender with the hazelnut butter | Blend until you have a really smooth chocolate spread

Roll out 1 sheet of the pastry on its paper over a baking sheet so that the short side is nearest you | Use a ruler to find the center of the top edge of the pastry, about 4¾ inches in from the corners | Cut the pastry into a tall, narrow triangle, slicing from the top diagonally to the bottom corners so that you're left with the rough shape of a Christmas tree | Peel the excess pastry from the sheet and set it to one side | Repeat with the second sheet of pastry to make 2 tree triangles | Use the scraps of excess pastry to cut out some small festive shapes

Spread a generous layer of the chocolate hazelnut spread over one of the triangles, leaving a ¹/₃-inch border all the way around. You will only need about half the chocolate mixture; store the rest in the fridge for spreading on toast ☺ | Brush all around the edge of the tree with milk | Pick up the second triangle of pastry and neatly lay it on top of the first tree | With your fingers, press together the edges of the pastry triangles to seal

Now make the branches of your tree | Leaving a ¾-inch margin in the middle of your tree, cut 8–10 horizontal slits along each side of the tree | Carefully lift one pastry branch and gently twist it to make a spiral | Repeat to twist all the branches

Put the dairy-free butter in a dish in the microwave and blast for a few seconds to melt (or melt in a small pan over medium heat) | Brush the melted butter all over the tree and any festive shapes | Put the baking sheet in the oven and bake for 20–25 minutes, until golden brown (smaller shapes may take less time so keep an eye on them) | Take the baking sheet out of the oven and let the tree cool to room temperature before moving it

Carefully transfer the tree to a serving board, dust with the powdered sugar, and serve

Pictured on pages 254–255

BREAKFASTS

Henry's favorite
Baby Croissants

Ian's favorite
Big Breakfast Bagel

BIG BREAKFAST BAGEL

This is a wonderfully indulgent, far healthier version of a fast-food classic. The real heroes are the eggplant bacon and scrambled tofu that work brilliantly in any breakfast-y recipe. The black salt adds an amazing eggy flavor to the scrambled tofu, which has a fantastic creamy texture. If you like things spicy, add half a chopped fresh green chili.

SERVES 4

4 bagels
a few chives, for garnish
4 slices dairy-free cheese
dairy-free butter, for spreading
ketchup, optional

FOR THE SCRAMBLED TOFU
1 (10 oz) block firm tofu
2 garlic cloves
3 scallions
1 (10½ oz) block silken tofu
2½ tbsp dairy-free butter
¼ tsp ground turmeric
1 tsp black pepper
1 tsp *kala namak* (black salt), optional

FOR THE EGGPLANT BACON
2 tbsp olive oil
1½ tbsp maple syrup
1 tbsp soy sauce
1 tsp smoked paprika
½ tsp garlic powder
½ tsp liquid smoke
1 small eggplant

Preheat oven to 320°F | Tofu press or 2 clean kitchen towels and a weight such as a heavy book | Line a sheet pan | Fine grater or Microplane | Food processor | Large skillet

Press the tofu using a tofu press or place it between two clean kitchen towels, lay it on a plate, and put a weight on top | Leave for 10–15 minutes to drain and firm up before you start cooking

Meanwhile, make the eggplant bacon | Put all the ingredients except for the eggplant into a mixing bowl and mix together with a fork | Cut the stem off the eggplant and slice the flesh lengthwise into quarters, then again to make 5mm-thick slices | Add to the marinade and carefully turn to coat | Transfer to the lined sheet pan and drizzle with any remaining marinade | Put the pan in the oven and bake for 40 minutes, turning halfway through

Meanwhile, cut the bagels in half | Snip the chives

Now make a start on the scrambled tofu | Peel and grate the garlic | Thinly slice the scallions | Place the silken tofu in the food processor and blitz to a smooth cream

Put the skillet over medium heat | Add the dairy-free butter and melt | Add the sliced scallions and stir for 3–5 minutes | Add the garlic and stir for 1 minute | Add the turmeric, black pepper, and *kala namak*, and stir them into the onions

Put the bagels in the toaster to toast

Back to the scrambled tofu | Drain any liquid from the pressed firm tofu | Pour the creamed silken tofu into the skillet and stir everything together | Once the silken tofu has taken on the color of the turmeric, crumble the firm tofu into the pan | Fold everything together for 1–2 minutes to completely warm through | Take the pan off the heat

Serve up | Butter the toasted bagels | Put 1 slice of dairy-free cheese on the bottom half of each bagel | Cover the cheese with equal portions of scrambled tofu | Take the pan out of the oven and top the scrambled tofu with the eggplant bacon slices | Squeeze over some ketchup, if using | Garnish with the chopped chives | Close the lids of the bagels and serve

BABY CROISSANTS

Henry LOVES chocolate croissants and has been working on a replacement ever since he stopped eating dairy. These are incredibly easy to make since they use store-bought pastry (we like easy recipes!). They taste great fresh from the oven and are fun to roll up with friends. You can make the almond mix the day before and store it in a covered bowl in the fridge.

ALMOND CROISSANTS

MAKES 12

1 (11 oz) sheet ready-rolled plant-based puff pastry
¼ cup superfine sugar
3 tbsp water
1 cup almond flour
½ cup + 2 tbsp powdered sugar, plus extra for dusting
1 tsp almond extract
¼ cup sliced almonds

Preheat oven to 390°F | Line 2 baking sheets with parchment paper | Large cutting board that will fit in your fridge | Small saucepan | Pastry brush

Unroll the pastry onto the cutting board, keeping it on its paper | Cut into 6 equal rectangles measuring roughly 3 × 7 inches by cutting the whole sheet in half crosswise and then cutting each half in three lengthwise | Cut each rectangle diagonally from corner to corner to create 12 long, thin triangles | Place the cutting board with the pastry in the fridge to chill

Meanwhile, make the syrup | Put the saucepan over medium heat | Pour in the superfine sugar and water and stir constantly until the sugar has dissolved and the liquid starts to bubble gently | Pour the syrup into a bowl and set aside to cool

Tip the almond flour and powdered sugar into a bowl and mix well | Add the almond extract and mix with a fork | Add 2 tablespoons of syrup and stir to make a smooth paste

Remove the chilled pastry from the fridge | Take an even tablespoon of the almond paste out of the bowl and place it at the wide end of one of the pastry triangles | Neatly roll up the pastry all the way to the end, forming a small croissant shape | Press down the edges of the pastry to seal tightly | Repeat to roll all your baby croissants

Place the croissants on the lined baking sheets, making sure they're well spaced out | Brush them all over with the remaining sugar syrup | Sprinkle the sliced almonds over the top | Place the baking sheets in the oven and bake the baby croissants for 20 minutes, until crispy and golden

Take the baking sheets out of the oven | Dust the croissants with a tiny bit of powdered sugar, transfer to a plate, and serve

CHOCOLATE CROISSANTS

MAKES 12

1 (11 oz) sheet ready-rolled plant-based
    puff pastry
¼ cup superfine sugar
3 tbsp water
3½ oz dark chocolate
3 tbsp powdered sugar
2 tbsp cocoa powder

Preheat oven to 390°F | **Line 2 baking sheets with parchment paper** | **Large cutting board that will fit in your fridge** | **Grater** | **Small saucepan** | **Pastry brush**

To make chocolate croissants, follow the method for Almond Croissants (opposite) to make the pastry triangles and sugar syrup

Grate the dark chocolate into a mixing bowl and sprinkle in the powdered sugar | Stir with a fork to combine and set to one side

Remove the chilled pastry from the fridge | Sprinkle the chocolate and powdered sugar mix evenly all over the pastry triangles | Neatly roll all the triangles, from the wide end to the thin end, into baby croissants

Place the croissants on the lined baking sheets, making sure they're well spaced out | Brush them with the sugar syrup and dust with the cocoa powder | Place the baking sheets in the oven and bake for 20 minutes, until crispy and golden

Take the baking sheets out of the oven | Transfer the baby croissants to a plate and serve

Pictured on pages 262–263

NUEVOS RANCHEROS

This is the perfect solution to the problem "I-want-a-hearty-breakfast-but-also-want-to-be-healthy." Chock-full of veggies and color and high in protein, it is hearty and filling. Feel free to have a play with the ingredients—add some mushrooms when you add the onions, or switch the potatoes to sweet potatoes.

SERVES 4

1 (10 oz) block firm tofu
10 oz new potatoes
1 red onion
1 green bell pepper
3 garlic cloves
5 tbsp olive oil
1 tbsp smoked paprika
1 tbsp ground cumin
1 tbsp ground coriander
1 tsp cayenne pepper
2 tsp salt
½ tsp black pepper
4 limes
1 lemon
1 (14.5 oz) can diced tomatoes
2 tsp chipotle paste (or hot sauce)
3½ oz kale
1 (14 oz) can black beans
16 cherry tomatoes
8 scallions
1 avocado
½ oz cilantro

Tofu press or 2 clean kitchen towels and a weight such as a heavy book | Saucepan of boiling water over high heat | Fine grater or Microplane | Skillet

. . . .

Press the tofu using a tofu press or place it between two clean kitchen towels, lay it on a plate, and put a weight on top | Leave for at least 30 minutes to drain and firm up before you start cooking

Meanwhile, cut the potatoes into ⅓-inch cubes | Tip them into the pan of boiling water, bring back up to a boil, and cook for 5 minutes | Drain in a colander and leave to rest for 5–10 minutes

Meanwhile, peel and finely dice the red onion | Cut the bell pepper in half, cut out the stem and seeds, and chop into ⅓-inch chunks | Peel and grate the garlic cloves

Warm the skillet over medium heat and add the oil | Add the cooked potatoes and chopped onions and fry for 5 minutes, stirring continuously | Add the garlic, paprika, cumin, ground coriander, cayenne pepper, salt, and pepper, continuing to stir gently | Add the green pepper and stir together well | Crumble in the pressed tofu and fold it into the rest of the ingredients

Cut 2 of the limes and the lemon in half and squeeze the juice into the pan, catching any seeds with your other hand | Pour in the diced tomatoes and chipotle paste and gently fold into the rest of the ingredients | Let everything simmer for 2 minutes

Remove the tough stems from the kale | Shred the leaves and add them to the pan | Drain and rinse the black beans and add them to the pan | Fold everything together and cook for another 5 minutes

Finely chop the tomatoes and scallions | Halve and carefully pit the avocado by tapping the pit firmly with the heel of a knife so that it lodges in the pit, then twist and remove | Scoop out the flesh with a spoon and cut into thin slices | Cut the remaining limes into wedges | Pull the leaves from the cilantro and discard the stems

Divide the cooked mixture among serving bowls | Top with the fresh vegetables and herbs | Serve with the lime wedges to squeeze over the top

LUSHY NUT BUTTER

Nothing can replace the taste of homemade nut butters. You can make the process quicker by skipping roasting the nuts, but the flavor will be a little less richly developed, so we recommend you roast them. Keep the butters in sterilized airtight containers—ideally jars with a rubber seal. They will keep in the fridge for up to a month.

MAKES 1 JAR (ABOUT 2¼ CUPS)

1 lb nuts; we use pecans, almonds, or peanuts
1–2 tbsp maple syrup
a pinch of salt
coconut oil or olive oil, optional

Preheat oven to 350°F | Baking sheet | Sterilized jar (see page 39) | Blender

Spread the nuts over the baking sheet | Put the sheet in the oven for 10 minutes | Remove and leave to cool to room temperature

Tip the nuts into the blender and blend for 6–12 minutes until smooth, pausing occasionally to scrape down the sides | Add 1 tablespoon of the maple syrup and the salt, put the lid back on, and blend for another 10 seconds | If yours doesn't come together into a butter and just looks like blended nuts, add a tiny bit of coconut oil or olive oil to loosen the mix | Taste and add more maple syrup if necessary, blending it in for a few seconds

Spoon into the sterilized jar and put the lid on | Store in the fridge

FRENCH TOAST

This breakfast is indulgent with a capital "I." You and your guests will find it hard to believe it isn't filled with butter! As well as the toppings below, try caramelized banana slices with a little cinnamon, or our nutty chocolate spread on page 252. Get ahead by making the batter the day before, keeping it in an airtight container in the fridge.

SERVES 4

7 tbsp all-purpose flour
2 tbsp superfine sugar
1 tsp ground cinnamon
1 cup unsweetened plant-based milk
3 tbsp maple syrup
8 tbsp dairy-free butter
8 slices thick white bread

TOPPINGS FOR PEANUT BUTTER & JAM
4 tbsp peanut butter
4 tbsp raspberry jam
5 oz fresh raspberries
4 tbsp chopped peanuts

TOPPINGS FOR SUMMER BERRIES
3½ oz fresh strawberries
5 oz fresh raspberries
3½ oz fresh blueberries
⅓ cup soy cream
¼ cup maple syrup

Preheat oven to 210°F | Baking sheet on the middle rack of the oven | Large skillet over medium heat | Line a plate with paper towels

First make the batter for the toasts | Put the flour, sugar, and cinnamon into a wide shallow bowl and mix together with a fork or small balloon whisk | Slowly add the plant-based milk, whisking continuously to make a batter | Whisk in the maple syrup

Now cook the bread | Add 1 tablespoon dairy-free butter to the skillet and let it melt | Lay a slice of bread in the batter, then turn it over so the whole slice is well covered | Lay the battered bread on one side of the pan and quickly repeat with a second slice | Fry for 3–5 minutes on each side until the toasts are slightly crispy and golden brown | Transfer to the plate lined with paper towels for 30 seconds to soak up the excess fat | Cut each slice in half to form triangles and transfer to the baking sheet to keep warm | Repeat to cook all the bread

PB&J FRENCH TOAST

Spread the French Toast triangles with peanut butter and raspberry jam | Sandwich the triangles together, scatter with the raspberries and peanuts, and serve

SUMMER BERRY FRENCH TOAST

Scatter the fresh strawberries, raspberries, and blueberries over the French Toasts | Drizzle with soy cream and maple syrup and serve

SHEET-PAN BREAKFAST

A one-pan English breakfast that will save you from all that washing up. This recipe is all about ease, so we use store-bought sausages, but you can also use our BOSH! Bangers on page 95. If you want to be a little more adventurous, add a dollop of hummus with harissa on the plate when you serve.

SERVES 4

8 plant-based sausages
2 tbsp olive oil
1 garlic bulb, optional
4 medium tomatoes
1 red onion
4 portobello mushrooms
a few sprigs fresh rosemary or thyme
7 oz baby spinach
2 (14 oz) cans baked beans
4 slices fresh bread
2 avocados
1 lime, optional
ketchup, for serving
salt and black pepper

Preheat oven to 390°F | Large sheet pan | Small baking dish

First get the sausages and veg roasting | Put the sausages, half the olive oil, and the garlic, if using, onto the sheet pan | Toss and sprinkle with a little salt and pepper

Cut the tomatoes in half | Peel the onion and cut it into 8 wedges | Add the onions to the pan along with the mushrooms, gill sides up, and tomatoes, cut sides up | Drizzle olive oil over everything | Remove the leaves from the herbs by running your thumb and forefinger from the top to the base of the stems (the leaves should easily come away) and sprinkle them over the ingredients | Place the pan in the oven and cook for 25 minutes, to get the sausages really nice and browned, turning them once halfway through

Toward the end of the cooking time, bring water to a boil | Put the spinach into a colander over the sink and pour on the boiling water | Add a little cool water so that it's cool enough to touch, then squeeze the leaves to remove excess water | Remove the pan from the oven and nestle the spinach leaves between the other ingredients

Pour the baked beans into the small baking dish and put it in the oven alongside the sheet pan | Bake for 5 minutes, until the beans are piping hot

Meanwhile, toast the bread and slice the avocados | Halve and carefully pit the avocados by tapping each pit firmly with the heel of a knife so that it lodges in the pit, then twist and remove | Slice the flesh neatly and transfer to a serving plate | Quarter the lime, if using, and squeeze the juice over the avocado slices

Remove the pan from the oven and divide all the ingredients among plates | Serve with ketchup

CINNAMON SWIRL PANCAKES

These pancakes are an absolute treat. Packed with cinnamon spice and sugary icing goodness, they make for an amazing breakfast or brunch. We dare you to not eat the whole batch by yourself! They're that fantastic. Don't worry if you don't have a proper piping bag. You can cut a hole in the end of a freezer bag and it will work just as well.

MAKES 12 BIG PANCAKES

3¾ cups all-purpose flour
2 tbsp baking powder
2 tsp salt
2 tsp vanilla extract
4¼ cups unsweetened almond milk
dairy-free butter, for frying

FOR THE CINNAMON MIX
8 tbsp dairy-free butter
1 cup light brown sugar
4 tbsp ground cinnamon

FOR THE ICING
2½ cups powdered sugar
3 tbsp maple syrup, plus more
   for drizzling
2 tbsp + 2 tsp water

Preheat oven to 170°F | Small pan, optional | Squeezy bottle or piping bag (or snip off the corner of a freezer bag) | Saucepan | Spatula | Clean kitchen towel

....

Start by making the pancake batter | Put the flour, baking powder, salt, vanilla, and almond milk into a bowl and whisk together | Pour into a measuring cup

To make the cinnamon mix, put the butter in the microwave for a few seconds to melt (or melt in a small pan over medium heat) | Pour the melted butter into a bowl along with the sugar and cinnamon and stir to combine | Leave to cool and then transfer to a squeezy bottle or piping bag

Put the ingredients for the icing into a bowl and beat until smooth

Now cook your pancakes! Place the saucepan over medium-high heat | Add ½ teaspoon dairy-free butter and allow it to melt | Use a piece of paper towel to spread the melted butter around so the pan is fully greased | When the pan is really hot, pour half a cup or a small ladle of pancake mix into the center | Quickly grab your cinnamon mix and squeeze an even, steady swirl from the center of the pancake spiraling out to the edge | Cook for about 3–4 minutes, during which time bubbles will appear on the top | Lift up the edge of the pancake with a spatula to check if it's cooked underneath—if it feels dry and looks golden brown, it's ready | Flip and cook the other side for 1 minute, until it is perfectly golden brown

Put the pancake on a plate, cover it with a kitchen towel, and put it in the oven | Repeat to make all the pancakes | Remove from the oven and stack 'em high on a plate | Drizzle artfully with the icing, then pour over lashings of maple syrup and serve

MAPLE & PECAN PASTRIES

Using store-bought pastry makes these incredibly easy—
just make sure your nuts are chopped really fine for the best
texture. Try experimenting with other nuts for a different
flavor profile. For something a little more festive, you could
also try adding a pinch of ground cloves and ground nutmeg.

MAKES 6

5 oz pecans
2 tbsp dairy-free butter
7½ tbsp light muscovado sugar
3 tbsp + ¼ tsp maple syrup
½ tsp vanilla extract
¼ tsp salt
1 (11 oz) sheet ready-rolled plant-based
    puff pastry
1 tsp ground cinnamon
2 tbsp unsweetened plant-based milk,
    plus extra for brushing
scant 7 tbsp powdered sugar

**Preheat oven to 350°F | Line a sheet pan | Large baking sheet
| Cooling rack | Pastry brush**

Spread the pecans over the lined sheet pan | Put the pan in the oven for
5–6 minutes | Take them out and let them cool

Meanwhile, make the filling for your pastries | Put the dairy-free butter,
light muscovado sugar, 3 tablespoons of the maple syrup, the vanilla
extract, and salt into a bowl and beat to a thick cream | Finely chop the
pecans and add them to the bowl | Fold everything together so that you
have a thick, nutty, caramel-colored filling

Roll out the pastry on to its paper on a large baking sheet | Cut the
pastry in half lengthwise to form two rectangles | Cut each rectangle
into 3 equal-sized smaller rectangles

Divide the filling mixture into six | Take one portion of filling and mold it
into a sausage shape | Place it in the middle of a pastry rectangle and fold
the pastry over the filling, crimping the edges with a fork to seal | Repeat
to make all the pastries | Take a sharp knife and make four decorative slits
across the top of each pastry, then brush the tops with the plant-based milk

Put the baking sheet in the oven for 25–30 minutes, or until the pastries
are crispy and golden brown

Meanwhile, make a glaze | Put the ground cinnamon, ¼ teaspoon
maple syrup, milk, and powdered sugar into a small bowl and mix with
a fork

Take the baking sheet out of the oven and transfer the cooked pastries
to a cooling rack | Drizzle the glaze over them | Leave to cool to room
temperature before serving

Eat the rainbow

There are so many different opinions about optimum human nutrition. We think writer Michael Pollan nailed it when he said, "Eat food, not too much, mostly plants."

Perhaps a less beautiful but more accurate phrase could be "Eat colorful food, not too much, mostly plants." It's really important to fill your body with different colors of fruit, veggies, and spices.

We're often asked by friends and family, whatever their diet choices, how they can eat more healthily. It's important to state that we're not dieticians or nutritionists, and if you have specific health issues then it's always advisable to see a doctor. But we do spend a lot of time working with and researching food and we believe everyone can be healthier by focusing their diet around more plants, whether you're veggie, vegan, or even a meat eater.

Here are our top tips for staying healthy while eating a plant-based or plant-focused diet.

Aim for 10 fruit and veggies a day
The 10 fruit and veg a day (which used to be 5-a-day) is a great place to start to ensure you're well on your way to hitting your nutrient goals.

Eat less processed food
The more you can eat food in its original form, the better. Although we love plant-based sausages, for example, they are processed, so we don't eat them all the time. If you are eating plants close to their original form, that's a good indicator that the meal is healthy.

Eat lots of dark green
Dark green vegetables like spinach, kale, broccoli, arugula, and chard are high in really important nutrients like iron, magnesium, and folate. An easy way to get ahead of the day is to cram loads of these (say 3½ oz) into a morning smoothie (check our meal prep Smoothie on page 206). If you're pressed for time you can easily get green smoothies on the go, although they'll never cram as much in as you would in your own blender at home.

Get lots of colors on your plate
To increase your nutritional intake further, try to vary the color of the fruit and veg you eat. Different plants contain different phytochemicals and micronutrients, which have different benefits to your body, so mix it up and eat the rainbow.

Make sure you get your plant protein

People always ask us where we get our protein from—and the answer? From plants! Nuts, peanut butter, tofu, beans, peas, chickpeas, seitan, quinoa, tempeh, lentils, seeds, soy milk, and oats are all great sources of plant-based protein, and all contain additional nutritional benefits.

Don't forget B12-rich foods

It's great that everyone's talking about B12—an essential B vitamin that is present in animal products and which we need to maintain healthy blood and a healthy nervous system. Everyone can be low on B12 (not just veggies). We get ours from B12-fortified plant-based oat milks, nutritional yeast, or yeast extracts like Marmite, and we also take a B12-fortified supplement.

Consume a range of vitamins and nutrients

Read up on nutrition and if you're really interested, you can include professional monitoring like blood tests into your routine—after all, if you spend money checking the oil in your car, why not do the same for your body? We both take omega-3 and omega-6, which are derived from algae, and occasionally we'll pop a multivitamin. We get our arms into the sun for vitamin D but other than that, we eat lots of color.

Think 80% healthy and 20% wicked

Our good friend Derek Sarno from Wicked Healthy said it well: "Eat 80% healthy and 20% wicked and you'll be 100% awesome." This book may lean slightly the other way, but just make sure you're eating greens and colorful plates most of the time and save the more decadent dishes, like our lasagna, for weekends and special occasions.

Swap to lower-GI carbs

Not all carbs are created equal. We are fine with eating carbohydrates and we're happy that this is a great and balanced way to live. But if you're a bit of a carbophobe, try swapping higher-GI, processed and refined carbs for lower-GI, less-processed options. Sweet potatoes are great, as are brown rice and whole-wheat pasta. They're higher in fiber, slower for your body to digest, and just generally better for you.

All hail home-cooked food

Comfort and "junk" food can be part of a healthy diet—especially if you cook them yourself! Dishes like our burgers, party poppers, or katsu curry may not be the healthiest, but they're delicious, and if you cook them yourself you know exactly what's gone into them. Plus, they're going to be much healthier than if you bought them in a fast-food joint.

Overall, it's important that we all think about our nutrition and take care of what we put into our bodies. Lots of water, not too much caffeine, not too much alcohol, and daily exercise are also important. These rules apply for everyone, whatever you eat.

Gratitude

Ta duckies

You for holding this book in your hands, we are grateful to be a part of your life, even if only for a moment! | Every single member of #teambosh, for sharing, commenting, and liking our videos and, most importantly, cooking our food! | Everyone who bought this book and our super-duper-bestselling-award-winning first book | Everyone who follows us on our social media channels—we exist because of you and we are completely, utterly, and eternally grateful for you, your time, and your attention | You are everything the Universe is doing right now | Go forth, be bold, do amazing things, we love you all

The creative team who spent weeks working on this beautiful book with us | Lizzie Mayson with Stephanie Mcleod for your truly exceptional photography and for making our food and faces look as sleek as possible | Frankie Unsworth for your incredible food styling and skills in the kitchen, as well as Izy Hossack & Hattie Arnold | Sarah Birks for your excellent prop styling and design skills | Saskia Quirke & Belle Jones for making us look super-duper fly | Paul Palmer-Edwards for your design mastery and love of lettering | Emily-Jane Williams for being the best makeup artist we've ever worked with

HQ / HarperCollins for putting this wonderful book together | Lisa Milton for being a total legend and a real champion for women | Rachel Kenny for being a visionary and bringing us into the family | Freddie Kenny for being cute AF | Kate Fox & Laura Herring for helping us turn our culinary creativity into written form, twice! | Also Caroline McArthur & Laura Nickoll | Charlie Redmayne for THOSE Jägerbombs and your belief in us, it means a lot | Sophie Calder for looking after us on the road | Louise McGrory for your excellent eye for design | Georgina Green for your hustle | All the rest of the passionate team including Jo Rose, Celia Lomas, Jess Htay, Jen Callahan-Packer, Hannah Sawyer, JP Hunting, Darren Shoffren, Samantha Luton, Ben

North | All the team at William Morrow—Cassie Jones, Anwesha Basu, Kara Zauberman & Benjamin Steinberg—for helping us bring our food to a huge and hungry Stateside audience

#Teambosh for helping us create a silly amount of recipes, given away for free on a daily basis, to help us empower the whole world to eat more plants | Cathy, Elsa & Charlie, thank you all for being bloody awesome. BOSH! wouldn't function without your graft | Clare Gray for your dietary expertise and mastery in the kitchen, and for creating wonderful food with us, like the Bakewell Tart and Wild West Wings | Jenna Leiter & Jordan Bourke for helping us refine and perfect our recipes and get them book-ready | EmJ for making our faces look pretty and for your amazing vegan bags | The mighty Bev James and Dave for your inspiration, friendship, and guidance | Carver PR, Megan, Jacob, Sarah & the gang for helping us reach the world | Ellie Brown for THAT CamemBOSH! recipe | Alexis Gauthier for the incredible Faux Gras | Rachel Hagreen for helping us find our style | Bodyweight D for the hours on the bars and the mats | Nicola Richman & Sophie Pryn for cooking up a storm with us | Sarah Durber for your friendship and hustle | Jeremy Roberts & team for your guidance | Natalie Maher from Pollitt & partners for your early help and art direction | Charles Lucas for your numerical wizardry | Guy Mottershead for your vision and belief | Amy Gladding for the arsenal of pots and pans!

Supporters, collaborators & co-conspirators | Damien & Judy @ Vevolution | Robbie, Klaus & Maria @ Plant-Based News | All the Veganuary crew | Anna Jones | Rupy Aujla | Dave & Steve (The Happy Pear) | Si & Dave (The Hairy Bikers) | Yotam Ottolenghi | Prue Leith | Brett Cobley (EpiVegan) | Gary Barlow | Ella Woodward (Deliciously Ella) | Morgan Masters | Ed Winters (Earthling Ed) | James Aspey | Tim Shieff & all the Ethcs crew | Paul Brown & the team at BOL

| JP, Alex, Anna & all the squad at allplants | Grace Regan | Venetia Falconer | All the Vegan Nights crew | The Soho House Group—a good portion of this book was written in your houses | Wilderness festival—you made memories that will never fade | Thanks to all the media, producers & TV execs who have supported us—we couldn't have done this without you | Dawn Carr & the team at PETA | All the lovely people at Mercy4Animals | Rachel Mills for having a good heart | Jamie Bolding & all the team at Jungle Creations for being epic people

Henry's fam | Jane & Mark | Alice & Graham | Bruce | Chris, Paul & Tom Williams | Sukey, Nick, Gus & Arthur | Claire, Nick & Xander | Alison & Curtis | John Dodd, Zoe & Stanley | Davey P

Ian's fam | Mum, Dad, Frances & Stew | Carolyn, Edward & Philip | Robin & Suzie | Simon | Josephine, Katie, Mike & Kev | Steve, Shirley, Lynsey & Kerry

The prosecco club fam & associates (you know who you are) | Alex & Tara | Leanne | Nat, Khairan & Lennox | Marcus, Ellie, Jasper & Caspian | Ekow,

Claire, Hugo & Xander | Zulf, Farhana, Ayza & Ayla | Alex Farbz, Cat, Freddie & Samuel | Addison, Claire & Stanley | Kweku & Angie | Tom, Emilie, Alex & Ruby | Martha, Duncan & Ernie | Josh, Charlotte, Leo & Bump | Tim, Susie & Wren | Nick & Ruth | Maso, Bex & Finn | Tom, Stef & Romy | Chris & Nikita | Luke & Kasia | Nish | Janey | Joe | Jenny | Lee | Louis | Mutty | Louisa | Sal | Tommy | Ben | AK

Our inspiration | Kip Anderson | Ed Winters | Pamela Anderson | Tim Shieff | James Aspey | Naturally Stefanie | Eco-Vegan Gal | Matthew Kenny | Derek & Chad Sarno (Wicked Healthy) | Greg "The Bodysmith" Smith | Jamie Oliver | Adam Biddle, Joe & the team at GH05T | Matthew Glover & Jane Land | All the restaurateurs, cafe owners, and street food traders who are showing the world that plant-based food is awesome | Gary Vaynerchuk | Tim Ferriss | Peter McKinnon | Casey Neistat | Dan Mace | Black Coffee | Jon Hopkins | Photek | Burial | Arctic Monkeys | Tiga & Kölsch | Maya Jane Coles | George Fitzgerald— *All That Must Be* was the official album playing nonstop during the creation of this book

INDEX

3-ingredient flatbreads 78

aioli 178
almonds
    almond croissants 260
    Bakewell tart 232–3
    one-pan pasanda 28
    orange, fennel &
        watercress salad 186
    romesco salad 202
American classic sandwich 41
American classics 19
apples: bún bò huế 68
applesauce: pulled jackfruit
    sandwich 92
apricots: roast sweet potato
    tagine 98
aquafaba
    homemade melty
        cheese 43
    mini banoffee meringues
        236
    mozzarella 102
    yule log 250
asparagus: easy tomato pasta
    with pan-grilled asparagus
    209
avocados
    giant BLT 87
    green chile guacamole 155
    guacajacks 47
    LA guacburger 51
    nuevos rancheros 265
    quick quesadillas 48
    sheet-pan breakfast 270

baba ganoush 197
bagels: big breakfast bagel
    258
baked beans: sheet-pan
    breakfast 270
Bakewell tart 232–3
balsamic onions 50
bananas
    banana bread blondies 231
    banana bread doughnuts
        214

banana chocolate swirl
    pie 224–5
banana split 248
banoffee with caramel
    sauce (ice cream) 217
mini banoffee meringues
    236
bang bang noodle salad 201
bangers in blankets 137
banoffee with caramel sauce
    (ice cream) 217
batata harra (spicy potatoes)
    196
BBQ beans with mushroom
    burnt ends 170
BBQ sauce 166
beans
    BBQ beans with mushroom
        burnt ends 170
    BOSH! bangers 95–6
    loaded potato nachos
        154–5
    nuevos rancheros 265
    piri piri protein lunchbox
        207
    rice & beans 205
    sheet-pan breakfast 270
bean sprouts: bún bò huế 68
béchamel sauce 91, 112
beet
    BOSH! bangers 95–6
    clementine roasted root
        vegetables 138
    faux gras 39
    roast beet mash 181
bell peppers
    chili jam 79
    curry house jalfrezi 74
    Holy Trinity Louisiana
        gumbo 80
    piri piri chorizo bake 60
    quick quesadillas 48
    romesco salad 202
    seaside roll with salsa
        verde & new potatoes 115
    sweet potato tikka masala
        88

berries, mixed: French toast
    269
bhajis: big bad bhajis with
    spicy tomato chutney 169
big bad bhajis with spicy
    tomato chutney 169
big breakfast bagel 258
biryani: Henry's biryani with
    cilantro chutney 121–2
black beans
    black bean guacamole 47
    guacajacks 47
    nuevos rancheros 265
    quick quesadillas 48
bok choy
    bún bò huế 68
    speedy hoisin mushrooms
        64
    spicy Thai salad 190
    Vietnamese sticky tofu 36
BOSH! bangers 95–6
BOSH! BBQ sauce 166
BOSH! burger sauce 50
BOSH! hacks 22
BOSH! quick custard 233
BOSH! Xmas (time plan)
    130–1
brandy: fruity sangria 145
bread. see also sandwiches
    3-ingredient flatbreads 78
    camembosh hedgehog 150
    dough 3ways 101
    French toast 269
    Ian's delightful daal & roti
        70–1
    kebabish tandoori special
        107
    kofta 195
    mega mezze platter 194–7
    quick quesadillas 48
    ultimate falafel wrap 77
British classics 18
broccauliflower cheese 54
broccoli: broccauliflower
    cheese 54
Brussels sprouts with maple
    mushrooms 137

bulgur wheat: tabbouleh 195
bún bò huế 68
burgers
    Ibiza sunset burger 50
    LA guacburger 51
buttercream filling:
    chocolate buttercream
    238
buttermilk marinade 165–6

cabbage
    crunchy cali slaw 177
    spicy Thai salad 190
Café de Paris secret sauce 117
cakes
    banana bread blondies 231
    banana bread doughnuts
        214
    chocolate mirror cake
        238–9
    classic Victoria sponge
        245
    lemon drizzle loaf cake 242
    maple & pecan pastries 274
    yule log 250
camembosh hedgehog 150
candied peanuts 248
cannellini beans
    BBQ beans with
        mushroom burnt ends
        170
    BOSH! bangers 95–6
caramel sauce 217, 236
carrots
    BOSH! bangers 95–6
    carrot crackling 92
    Christmas crisscross
        134–5
    clementine roasted root
        vegetables 138
    crunchy cali slaw 177
    homemade melty
        cheese 43
    one-pan pasanda 28
    roasted root vegetables
        126
cashew cream 236

cashew nuts
  banoffee with caramel
    sauce (ice cream) 217
  camembosh hedgehog 150
  cashew cream 236
  classic chocolate (ice
    cream) 216
  clean slate vanilla (ice
    cream) 218
  homemade melty
    cheese 43
  mozzarella 102
  New York–style baked
    strawberry cheesecake
    222
  raspberry ripple cookie
    crumble 218
  soft whipped cream 249
  sour cream 155
  spinach & ricotta
    zucchinioli 193
cauliflower
  broccauliflower cheese 54
  kebabish tandoori special
    107
  one-pan pasanda 28
celery
  Christmas crisscross 134–5
  Holy Trinity Louisiana
    gumbo 80
cheeky mango lassi 145
cheese, dairy-free
  American classic sandwich
    41
  big breakfast bagel 258
  broccauliflower cheese 54
  camembosh hedgehog 150
  cheeseburger dough balls
    104
  English ploughman's
    sandwich 42
  homemade melty
    cheese 43
  loaded potato nachos
    154–5
  mozzarella 102
  quick quesadillas 48

  spinach & ricotta
    zucchinioli 193
cheeseburger dough balls
  104
cheesecake: New York–style
  baked strawberry
  cheesecake 222
cherries: Bakewell tart 232–3
chestnuts
  Christmas crisscross
    134–5
  ultimate nut roast 128
chickpeas
  falafel 78
  homemade turmeric
    hummus 208
  kofta 195
  lemon & cilantro hummus
    196
  roast sweet potato
    tagine 98
chilies
  chili jam 79
  green chile guacamole 155
  homemade chili oil 47
  homemade sambal chili
    sauce 208
  Wild West hot sauce 161
chocolate
  banana bread blondies 231
  banana chocolate swirl
    pie 224–5
  chocolate croissants 261
  chocolate mirror cake
    238–9
  chocolate syrup 248
  classic chocolate (ice
    cream) 216
  New York-style baked
    strawberry cheesecake
    222
  notella Christmas tree
    252–3
  yule log 250
chorizo sausages
  eazy chorizo 61
  piri piri chorizo bake 60

Christmas & Thanksgiving 17
  bangers in blankets 137
  BOSH! Xmas (time plan)
    130–1
  Brussels sprouts with
    maple mushrooms 137
  Christmas crisscross 134–5
  clementine roasted root
    vegetables 138
  crispy, fluffy, perfect roast
    potatoes 141
  notella Christmas tree
    252–3
  perfect gravy 143
  Thanksgiving salad 189
  ultimate roast stuffing
    balls 142
  yule log 250
chutneys 21
  cilantro chutney 122
  English ploughman's
    sandwich 42
  spicy tomato chutney 169
cilantro chutney 122
cinnamon swirl pancakes
  273
classic chocolate (ice cream)
  216
classic lasagna 112
classic Victoria sponge 245
clean slate vanilla (ice cream)
  218
clementine roasted root
  vegetables 138
cocktails 144–6
  cheeky mango lassi 145
  fruity sangria 145
  naughty agua fresca 144
  strawberry daiquiri slushy
    144
coconut milk
  banana chocolate swirl
    pie 224–5
  Ian's delightful daal & roti
    70–1
  mini banoffee meringues
    236

one-pan pasanda 28
  soft whipped cream 249
  sweet potato tikka masala
    88
  tom kha 35
coconut water: Vietnamese
  sticky tofu 36
coconut yogurt
  tzatziki 58
  Wild West wings 160
cookies
  Empire biscuits 228
  super-simple shortbread
    228
corn
  crunchy carnival salad
    205
  quick quesadillas 48
couscous: lemon & almond
  couscous 98
cream: soft whipped cream
  249
crispy, fluffy, perfect roast
  potatoes 141
croissants 260–1
crunchy cali slaw 177
crunchy carnival salad 205
cucumbers
  kebabish tandoori special
    107
  tabbouleh 195
  tzatziki 58
curries 16
  curry house jalfrezi 74
  Henry's biryani with
    cilantro chutney 121–2
  one-pan pasanda 28
  sweet potato tikka masala
    88
curry house jalfrezi 74
custard: BOSH! quick
  custard 233

daal: Ian's delightful daal &
  roti 70–1
De la Seoul hot sauce 161
dipping sauce 153

dips 21
    aioli 178
    baba ganoush 197
    dipping sauce 153
    green chile guacamole 155
    guacamole 51
    homemade turmeric
        hummus 208
    lemon & cilantro hummus
        196
    mint raita 107
    quick turmeric hummus 207
    satay sauce 158
    sour cream 155
    tzatziki 58
double-cooked rosemary
    fries with quick aioli 178
dough 3 ways 101
dough balls: cheeseburger
    dough balls 104
doughnuts: banana bread
    doughnuts 214
dressings 20
    bang bang peanut
        dressing 201
    crunchy cali slaw 177
    orange, fennel &
        watercress salad 186
    romesco salad 202
    satay dressing 158
    spicy Thai salad 190
    Thanksgiving salad 189
drinks. see cocktails

easy peasy roast dinner 123
easy tomato pasta with
    pan-grilled asparagus 209
eazy chorizo 61
eggplants
    baba ganoush 197
    bangers in blankets 137
    big breakfast bagel 258
    curry house jalfrezi 74
    eggplant katsu 57
Empire biscuits 228
English ploughman's
    sandwich 42
equipment 12

falafel 78
    ultimate falafel wrap 77
faux gras 39
fennel: orange, fennel &
    watercress salad 186
flatbreads
    3-ingredient flatbreads
        78
    kebabish tandoori special
        107
    ultimate falafel wrap 77
frangipane: Bakewell tart
    232−3
fries: double-cooked
    rosemary fries with quick
    aioli 178
fruit 17, 278−9
fruity sangria 145

giant BLT 87
gravies 20
    perfect gravy 143
    quick onion gravy 97
    red wine gravy 127
Greek gyros 58
green beans
    one-pan pasanda 28
    tom kha 35
green breakfast smoothies
    206
green chili guacamole 155
guacajacks 47
guacamole 51
    black bean guacamole 47
    green chili guacamole
        155
gumbo: Holy Trinity
    Louisiana gumbo 80

hash browns 51
hazelnuts
    notella Christmas tree
        252−3
    romesco salad 202
    ultimate nut roast 128
Henry's biryani with cilantro
    chutney 121−2
herb oil 127, 150

Holy Trinity Louisiana
    gumbo 80
homemade chili oil 47
homemade melty cheese 43
homemade sambal chili
    sauce 208
hot sauce
    De la Seoul hot sauce 161
    hot sauce 68
    Wild West hot sauce 161
hummus
    homemade turmeric
        hummus 208
    lemon & cilantro hummus
        196
    quick turmeric hummus
        207
    ultimate falafel wrap 77

Ian's delightful daal & roti 70−1
Ibiza sunset burger 50
ice cream 216−18
    banana split 248
    banoffee with caramel
        sauce 217
    classic chocolate 216
    clean slate vanilla 218
    knickerbocker glory 247
    raspberry ripple cookie
        crumble 218
icing
    chocolate buttercream 238
    chocolate frosting 250
    chocolate mirror glaze
        238
    quick icing 214
incredible mash 96
Indian-style chutney
    sandwich 42
Italian flavors 16

jackfruit
    easy peasy roast dinner 123
    Henry's biryani with
        cilantro chutney 121−2
    pulled jackfruit 126
    pulled jackfruit sandwich 92
jam: chili jam 79

kale
    green breakfast smoothies
        206
    Thanksgiving salad 189
kebabish tandoori special
    107
kidney beans
    Holy Trinity Louisiana
        gumbo 80
    rice & beans 205
knickerbocker glory 247
kofta 195

LA guacburger 51
lasagna: classic lasagna 112
lassi: cheeky mango lassi 145
lemons
    lemon & cilantro hummus
        196
    lemon drizzle loaf cake
        242
lentils
    faux gras 39
    Ian's delightful daal & roti
        70−1
    pan-fried seitan steak with
        secret sauce 116
    shepherd's pie 108
    Thanksgiving salad 189
loaded potato nachos
    154−5
lushy nut butter 266

mangoes: cheeky mango
    lassi 145
maple & pecan pastries 274
margherita pizza 102
marinades
    bangers in blankets 137
    buttermilk marinade
        165−6
    quick spicy marinade 207
    tandoori marinade 107
mashy mashy peas 84
Mediterranean goodness 19
mega mezze platter 194−7
meringues: mini banoffee
    meringues 236

milk, plant-based
    BOSH! quick custard 233
    cinnamon swirl pancakes
        273
    green breakfast smoothies
        206
    ice cream 216–18
mini banoffee meringues
    236
mini mushroom pies 91
mozzarella: margherita pizza
    102
mushrooms
    bang bang noodle salad 201
    BBQ beans with
        mushroom burnt ends
        170
    Brussels sprouts with
        maple mushrooms 137
    bún bò hué 68
    Christmas crisscross 134–5
    classic lasagna 112
    faux gras 39
    Greek gyros 58
    Holy Trinity Louisiana
        gumbo 80
    mini mushroom pies 91
    sheet-pan breakfast 270
    shepherd's pie 108
    speedy hoisin mushrooms
        64
    tom kha 35
    ultimate nut roast 128
    Wild West wings 160
mustard mash 181

nachos: loaded potato
    nachos 154–5
naughty agua fresca 144
New York-style baked
    strawberry cheesecake 222
noodles
    bang bang noodle salad
        201
    bún bò hué 68
nori: sushi cupcakes 153
notella Christmas tree
    252–3

Notting Hill patties 173
nuevos rancheros 265
nutrition 279
nuts. see also individual nuts
    lushy nut butter 266
    ultimate nut roast 128

oil
    herb oil 127, 150
    homemade chili oil 47
one-pan pasanda 28
onions
    balsamic onions 50
    big bad bhajis with spicy
        tomato chutney 169
    Holy Trinity Louisiana
        gumbo 80
    quick onion gravy 97
    quick red onion pickle 107
orange, fennel & watercress
    salad 186

pan-fried seitan steak with
    secret sauce 116
pancakes: cinnamon swirl
    pancakes 273
parsnips
    BOSH! bangers 95–6
    roasted root vegetables 126
    ultimate nut roast 128
    ultimate roast stuffing
        balls 142
party poppers with BOSH!
    BBQ sauce 165–6
pasta: easy tomato pasta
    with pan-grilled asparagus
        209
pastries, maple & pecan 274
pâté: faux gras 39
peaches: fruity sangria 145
peanut butter
    banana bread blondies 231
    French toast 269
peanuts
    bang bang noodle salad
        201
    candied peanuts 248
    spicy Thai salad 190

peas
    mashy mashy peas 84
    tofish finger sandwich 83
pecans
    banana chocolate swirl pie
        224–5
    Christmas crisscross 134–5
    maple & pecan pastries 274
    Thanksgiving salad 189
    ultimate nut roast 128
perfect gravy 143
piri piri protein lunchbox 207
pesto 193
pickles
    Indian-style chutney
        sandwich 42
    quick red onion pickle 107
pies
    Bakewell tart 232–3
    banana chocolate swirl pie
        224–5
    Christmas crisscross 134–5
    mini mushroom pies 91
    notella Christmas tree
        252–3
    Notting Hill patties 173
    seaside roll with salsa
        verde & new potatoes 115
pineapple
    bún bò hué 68
    naughty agua fresca 144
piri piri chorizo bake 60
pita bread: Greek gyros 58
pizzas: margherita pizza 102
planning 24
platters: mega mezze platter
    194–7
popcorn bites: party poppers
    with BOSH! BBQ sauce
    165–6
port: perfect gravy 143
potatoes
    batata harra (spicy
        potatoes) 196
    crispy, fluffy, perfect roast
        potatoes 141
    double-cooked rosemary
        fries with quick aioli 178

hash browns 51
incredible mash 96
loaded potato nachos
    154–5
mustard mash 181
nuevos rancheros 265
roast beet mash 181
roasted root vegetables 126
seaside roll with salsa
    verde & new potatoes
    115
shepherd's pie 108
Texan potato salad 174
turbo tortilla 31
protein 18
pulled jackfruit 126
pulled jackfruit sandwich 92

quesadillas: quick quesadillas
    48
quick icing 214, 228
quick marinara sauce 102
quick onion gravy 97
quick quesadillas 48
quick red onion pickle 107
quick salsa 155
quick turmeric hummus 207

raspberries
    Bakewell tart 232–3
    banana split 248
    classic Victoria sponge 245
    knickerbocker glory 247
    raspberry ripple cookie
        crumble 218
    raspberry syrup 249
red wine gravy 127
refried beans: loaded potato
    nachos 154–5
rhubarb: poached rhubarb 233
rice
    BOSH! bangers 95–6
    curry house jalfrezi 74
    eggplant katsu 57
    Henry's biryani with
        cilantro chutney 121–2
    Holy Trinity Louisiana
        gumbo 80

piri piri protein lunchbox 207

piri piri chorizo bake 60

rice & beans 205

speedy hoisin mushrooms 64

sushi cupcakes 153

sweet potato tikka masala 88

Vietnamese sticky tofu 36

rice paper: satay summer rolls 158

roast beet mash 181

roast sweet potato mash 180

roast sweet potato tagine 98

roasted root vegetables 126

rolls: satay summer rolls 158

romesco salad 202

roti: Ian's delightful daal & roti 70–1

rum

    cheeky mango lassi 145

    strawberry daiquiri slushy 144

salads

    bang bang noodle salad 201

    crunchy cali slaw 177

    crunchy carnival salad 205

    orange, fennel & watercress salad 186

    romesco salad 202

    spicy Thai salad 190

    tabbouleh 195

    Texan potato salad 174

    Thanksgiving salad 189

salsas 21

    quick salsa 155

    salsa verde 115

sandwiches

    American classic sandwich 41

    English ploughman's sandwich 42

    giant BLT 87

    Indian-style chutney sandwich 42

pulled jackfruit sandwich 92

tofish finger sandwich 83

sangria: fruity sangria 145

satay sauce 158

satay summer rolls 158

sauces 20

    béchamel sauce 91, 112

    BOSH! BBQ sauce 166

    BOSH! burger sauce 50

    Café de Paris secret sauce 117

    caramel sauce 217, 236

    cheesy 54

    chili sauce 68

    curry sauce 88

    De la Seoul hot sauce 161

    dipping sauce 153

    homemade sambal chili sauce 208

    katsu sauce 57

    piri piri sauce 60

    quick marinara sauce 102

    raspberry sauce 218

    satay sauce 158

    speedy tartar sauce 84

    spicy Thai salad 190

    super-speedy spaghetti 32

    Wild West hot sauce 161

sausages

    bangers in blankets 137

    BOSH! bangers 95–6

    cheeseburger dough balls 104

    eazy chorizo 61

    Notting Hill patties 173

    piri piri chorizo bake 60

    sheet-pan breakfast 270

seaside roll with salsa verde & new potatoes 115

seitan steak: pan-fried seitan steak with secret sauce 116

    sheet-pan breakfast 270

shepherd's pie 108

Singapore fried vermicelli 44

slaws: crunchy cali slaw 177

smoothies: green breakfast smoothies 206

soft whipped cream 249

soup

    bún bò hué 68

    tom kha 35

sour cream 155

Southeast Asian deliciousness 16

spaghetti: super-speedy spaghetti 32

speedy hoisin mushrooms 64

speedy tartar sauce 84

spicy Thai salad 190

spicy tomato chutney 169

spinach

    broccauliflower cheese 54

    green breakfast smoothies 206

    piri piri protein lunchbox 207

    sheet-pan breakfast 270

    spinach & ricotta zucchinioli 193

    ultimate falafel wrap 77

squash: Thanksgiving salad 189

strawberries

    banana split 248

    fruity sangria 145

    knickerbocker glory 247

    naughty agua fresca 144

    New York–style baked strawberry cheesecake 222

    strawberry daiquiri slushy 144

stuffing

    pulled jackfruit sandwich 92

    ultimate roast stuffing balls 142

super-simple shortbread 228

super-speedy spaghetti 32

sushi cupcakes 153

sweet potatoes

    crunchy carnival salad 205

    guacajacks 47

    piri piri chorizo bake 60

    roast sweet potato mash 180

roast sweet potato tagine 98

sweet potato tikka masala 88

syrup

    chocolate syrup 248

    raspberry syrup 249

tabbouleh 195

tagine: roast sweet potato tagine 98

takeout classics 17

tandoori marinade 107

tartar sauce

    speedy tartar sauce 84

    tofish finger sandwich 83

Tex-Mex 18

Texan potato salad 174

Thanksgiving salad 189

toast: French toast 269

tofish finger sandwich 83

tofu

    big breakfast bagel 258

    giant BLT 87

    New York–style baked strawberry cheesecake 222

    nuevos rancheros 265

    piri piri protein lunchbox 207

    satay summer rolls 158

    seaside roll with salsa verde & new potatoes 115

    tofish finger sandwich 83

    Vietnamese sticky tofu 36

tom kha 35

tomatoes

    BBQ beans with mushroom burnt ends 170

    chili jam 79

    Christmas crisscross 134–5

    classic lasagna 112

    easy tomato pasta with pan-grilled asparagus 209

    giant BLT 87

    guacajacks 47

    Ian's delightful daal & roti 70–1

kebabish tandoori special 107

loaded potato nachos 154–5

margherita pizza 102

Notting Hill patties 173

nuevos rancheros 265

piri piri chorizo bake 60

quick quesadillas 48

quick salsa 155

roast sweet potato tagine 98

romesco salad 202

sheet-pan breakfast 270

spicy tomato chutney 169

super-speedy spaghetti 32

tabbouleh 195

tom kha 35

toppings 155

   green chili guacamole 155

   quick salsa 155

   sour cream 155

tortillas: quick quesadillas 48

turbo tortilla 31

tzatziki: Greek gyros 58

ultimate falafel wrap 77

ultimate nut roast 128

ultimate roast stuffing balls 142

vegetables 17, 19, 278–9

   bang bang noodle salad 201

   classic lasagna 112

   clementine roasted root vegetables 138

   crunchy carnival salad 205

   easy peasy roast dinner 123

   Holy Trinity Louisiana gumbo 80

   perfect gravy 143

   roasted root vegetables 126

   satay summer rolls 158

   Singapore fried vermicelli 44

   spicy Thai salad 190

   sushi cupcakes 153

   turbo tortilla 31

vermicelli

   satay summer rolls 158

   Singapore fried vermicelli 44

Vietnamese sticky tofu 36

vitamin B12: 279

vodka: naughty agua fresca 144

walnuts

   clementine roasted root vegetables 138

   faux gras 39

   ultimate nut roast 128

   ultimate roast stuffing balls 142

watercress: orange, fennel & watercress salad 186

wheat gluten

   pan-fried seitan steak with secret sauce 116

   party poppers with BOSH! BBQ sauce 165–6

Wild West wings 160

wine

   fruity sangria 145

   red wine gravy 127

yogurt, dairy-free: cheeky mango lassi 145

yule log 250

zucchini

   kofta 195

   spinach & ricotta zucchinioli 193